Heidelberg Catechism

ℰℐ

Modern English Version

450th Anniversary Edition

The Reformed Church
in the United States
2013

COPYRIGHT

℀

For contact and other information
about the Reformed Church in the U.S.
www.rcus.org

Set in Adobe Jenson Pro

Contents

Catechismus

Oder
Christlicher Underricht /
wie der in Kirchen vnd Schulen der Churfürstlichen
Pfaltz getrieben
wirdt.

Gedruckt in der Churfürstlichen Stad Heydelberg / durch
Johannem Mayer.

1 5 6 3.

INTRODUCTION

ℬℭ

THE HEIDELBERG CATECHISM is one of the finest fruits of the Reformation. It epitomizes its essential teaching and has been proven in the fire of affliction. Holding forth Jesus Christ as our only comfort in life and in death, it presents very personally and eloquently what is necessary to know that we may live and die in that comfort. Today, those who are yearning for a beautiful statement of biblical truth will find this work a treasure. It remains as fresh as when it was first published 450 years ago and continues to hold a treasured place in the bosom of Reformed churches throughout the world.

Its value and appeal can be attributed to at least four factors. *First* and foremost is its intrinsic merit as a summary of biblical truth embodying the simplicity and profundity of Scriptural teaching. It crystalized the Christian faith as understood by the Reformed reformers of the sixteenth century, especially John Calvin. It also demonstrated continuity with the early church in its threefold structure of the creed, the law, and prayer.

Second, the catechism was beautifully designed to implement a Reformed course of training for both youth and adults. Though sometimes seen as a fault, the length of the catechism allowed it to provide a summary treatment of the full range of doctrine. Its language and rhythm of questions and answers endeared itself to those who sought an articulation of consistently biblical theology, and its division into Lord's Days provided an orderly method of instruction.

Third, this common tool of instruction enabled the Reformed movement to spread a unified theology. The endorsement of the catechism by consistories and synods in Germany, the Netherlands, Hungary, and Switzerland established it as one of the defining documents of the Reformed Reformation. The approval of the Synod of Dordrecht (1618–19) made it a standard of faith for Reformed Christians.

Fourth, because of these factors, congregations have diligently implemented the teaching of the catechism as an essential part of Christian training. It is unlikely that the Catechism would have had lasting significance unless innumerable pastors and teachers down through the centuries had implemented its use in the regular ministry of the church.

Contents and Structure

The purpose of the Heidelberg is seen in its original title: "Catechism or Instruction in Christian Doctrine, as it is conducted by the Churches and Schools of the Electoral Palatinate" (*Catechismus Oder Christlicher Underricht, wie der in Kirchen und Schulen der Churfürstlichen Pfaltz getrieben wirdt*). It follows a question–and–answer format to help the student come to a clear understanding of basic biblical doctrines. The Reformed church has historically emphasized the necessity of training and encouraging its youth to embrace the Christian faith. For this reason, those who have been baptized are called to use this catechism to prepare to confess their faith and become communicant members of the church of Jesus Christ.

The grand theme is stated in the answer to the first question, "What is your only comfort in life and in death?"

> That I, with body and soul, both in life and in death, am not my own, but belong to my faithful Savior Jesus Christ, who with His precious blood has fully satisfied for all my sins, and redeemed me from all the power of the devil; and so preserves me that without the will of my Father in heaven not a hair can fall from my head; indeed, that all things must work together for my salvation. Wherefore, by His Holy Spirit, He also assures me of eternal life, and makes me heartily willing and ready from now on to live unto Him.

This Trinitarian confession reflects Ephesians 1 and the church's early creeds. Its order follows the church's traditional use of the Apostles' Creed, the Ten Commandments, and the Lord's Prayer. But it integrates these three by using the pattern Paul provides in his Epistle to the Romans—condemnation, justification, and sanctification. Question 2 describes the resulting threefold structure of the catechism:

> How many things are necessary for you to know, that in this comfort you may live and die happily? Three things: *First*, the greatness of my sin and misery. *Second*, how I am redeemed from all my sins and misery. *Third*, how I am to be thankful to God for such redemption.

The well-known alliterations—Sin, Salvation, and Service; or, Guilt, Grace, and Gratitude—make this structure easy to remember.

The Heidelberg is infused with an understanding of the invincible grace of the Triune God. It fully affirms the key Reformation teaching of justification by faith alone through the imputation of Christ's righteousness. But it speaks of this in the context of the whole scope of God's sovereign grace.

Historical Background

The catechism received its name "Heidelberg" from the old capital city of the German lower Palatinate and its noted university. The founding of this seat of learning dates back to the year 1385.

The Reformation of the sixteenth century did not immediately find favor in the Palatinate, although Martin Luther (1483–1546) had been heard in Heidelberg as early as 1518. The university was connected to the Church of Rome, and it was difficult for anyone to take another position than that of hostility to the Reformation. The government also remained apathetic, fearing turmoil and change.

Nevertheless, the impact of reformation found its mark. On Sunday, December 20, 1545, when the mass was about to be celebrated at the principal church of Heidelberg, the people began singing the Reformation hymn, "To Us Salvation Now is Come" (*Es ist das Heil uns kommen her*). But the struggle for church reformation lasted another ten years, when finally the Peace of Augsburg (1555) established religious freedom. Sapience College (College of Wisdom), dedicated to the education of ministers, was soon opened in the Augustinian convent at Heidelberg.

The following decade, however, proved critical for the reform movement. The followers of Luther were divided among themselves: the ultra-Lutherans maintained the bodily presence of the Lord in the sacrament, while the followers of his associate, Philip Melanchthon (1497–1560), held to Christ's spiritual presence, as was taught by Calvin. The Palatinate, and especially Heidelberg, became the very battleground for these and other factions. Lutheran doctrine eventually became fixed in the Formula of Concord, while the Calvinistic influence became embodied in the Heidelberg Catechism. Three figures played an important role in this transformation.

Frederick III

In 1559, the electoral power of the Palatinate passed into the hands of Frederick III, who may truly be called the father of the Heidelberg Catechism. He determined to carry out the Reformation among his people without compromise. This meant that in the Palatinate, Christianity would be ordered and established both in regard to doctrine and worship, following the more thoroughly biblical views of the Reformed faith. For this reason, it was made mandatory that only the scriptural words of the institution of the Lord's Supper were to be used in the celebration of the Supper. All crosses, candles, altars, and pictures were removed from the churches, and the singing of the

Psalms in the German language was introduced. Contentious teachers and ministers were dismissed, and those of Reformed persuasion were called to fill the pulpit and the lectern. It was in this context that two able young men, Caspar Olevianus and Zacharias Ursinus, came to Heidelberg.

Caspar Olevianus

Caspar Olevianus, born on August 10, 1532, in the city of Treves, applied himself diligently to his studies. After attending various schools, he studied jurisprudence at the University of Bourges. One of his schoolmates was a son of Frederick III. Tragically, this promising young man and two other students drowned when their boat overturned while they attempted to cross a river. Olevianus tried to rescue his friend, almost losing his own life in the attempt. Then and there he vowed to dedicate his life to the ministry of the gospel.

Upon finishing his studies he traveled to Geneva, Switzerland, and attended the lectures of the renowned theologian John Calvin. At Zurich he made the acquaintance of Heinrich Bullinger and Peter Martyr Vermigli, and at Lausanne, Theodore Beza.

It was the zealous reformer William Farel, along with Calvin and Viret, who prevailed upon Olevianus to return to his homeland to preach. In 1559, at the age of twenty-seven, he returned to Treves where he took charge of a school and also began preaching with fearless zeal. Treves was thrown into commotion, and Olevianus and other reform leaders were cast into prison. After ten months of negotiations, they were set free under condition of heavy fines and banishment from the city. Caspar's character had been tempered in the furnace of persecution as the Lord prepared him for a much greater task.

Frederick III, recalling that Olevianus had risked his life to save his son, and realizing that he was now being persecuted and banished for the sake of the gospel, called him to Heidelberg. In 1560, he became lecturer at the university and professor of dogmatics. Within a year, however, he exchanged his position for the pastorate of a city church. Olevianus was eminently qualified and called by Christ to play a key role in the dissemination of Reformed doctrine by means of a new catechism.

Zacharias Ursinus

Zacharias Ursinus, born at Breslau, Silesia, on July 18, 1534, entered the University of Wittenberg, Germany, at the age of sixteen. He remained there for seven years, during which he became strongly attached to his eminent teacher, Philip Melanchthon. After this he made personal contact with leaders of the Reformation at Heidelberg and Strassburg in Germany; and at Basel, Lausanne, and Geneva in Switzerland.

In 1558, he became the rector (headmaster) of the Elizabethan "gymnasium," or high-school, at Breslau and found himself in the midst of an intense debate about whether Christ was materially or spiritually present in the elements of the Lord's Supper. From the beginning, Ursinus reflected the views of his teacher, Melanchthon, and for this reason the ire of the ultra-Lutherans rose against him, and he was branded a Calvinist. He ably defended his teaching on the sacraments and the person of Christ in a published tract, which did not bridge the differences as he had hoped, but only increased the antagonism. Early in 1560 he resigned his position, resolving,

> I will go to the Zurichers, whose reputation indeed is not great here, but who have so famous a name among other churches that it cannot be obscured by our preachers. They are God-fearing, thoroughly learned men with whom I have resolved to spend my life. God will provide for the rest.

Arriving at Zurich, he renewed his friendship with Bullinger and Vermigli. In God's providence Frederick III had just requested Vermigli to assist in the Reformation in the Palatinate. Considering himself too old for such a difficult task, he recommended instead his capable young friend, Ursinus. Thus the young theologican was called to Heidelberg in 1561 and became professor of theology at the university and also rector (chancellor) of Sapience College.

For many years Ursinus labored at these Christian institutions of learning, a very exacting scholar in his studies and lectures, yet always clear and concise in his presentation. For this reason he was eminently prepared for a leading role in preparing a new catechism.

Publication and Reception

In the German Palatinate, numerous catechisms were already in use, in fact, too many—their very number caused endless confusion, and none received any general and whole-hearted approval. It became apparent, therefore, that a catechism was needed that would be comprehensive, in which all the key doctrines would be clearly stated, and yet be so simple that even children could grasp the truths of salvation.

Frederick III entrusted his theologians and pastors with the preparation of a clear, concise, and popular statement of Christian doctrine in catechetical form which could be used in the home, church, and school. The preliminary work was done by the faculty of the university, but the final form and its editing was entrusted to Olevianus and Ursinus.

The finished manuscript, presented toward the close of the year 1562, received the hearty approval of the entire faculty and also of the pastors and teachers. It was submitted to the Synod, meeting at Heidelberg, and a resolution was passed to publish it immediately by government authority. The first edition of the new catechism came off the press with a preface by Frederick III dated January 19, 1563. The second and third editions, with minor additions along with a Latin translation, were published later in 1563. Beginning in the third edition, it was divided into fifty-two Lord's Days so that it might be explained each year. The fourth edition, published on November 15, 1563, as part of the the Palatinate Church Order (*Kirchenordnung*), is regarded as the standard text.

The spread and influence of this small book within the bounds of the Palatinate and in other areas of Europe exceeded all expectations, being welcomed by the Reformed everywhere. It was made mandatory in all the schools and churches of the Palatinate to teach it and to read it from the pulpit every Sunday according to its Lord's Days. Catechetical preaching and exposition were instituted for the Sunday afternoon service. All education, whether in the home, in the schools, or at the university was based upon it, and the theological training of students for the ministry centered around it. At Sapience College, Ursinus immediately began lectures on its contents which were later published.

The Catechism was soon adopted by the Dutch Synod of Wesel in 1568, by the Synod of Dort in 1571, and by the great ecumenical Synod of Dort in 1618–19. The British delegates at the Synod of Dort agreed that neither in their own nor in the French Church was there a catechism so suitable and excellent. They remarked, "Our Reformed brethren on the continent have a little book whose single leaves are not to be bought with tons of gold."

Besides the original Latin version, translations into Dutch by Petrus Dathenus and into Saxon-German appeared within a year of its original publication. These were followed by translations into English and Hungarian in 1567, French in 1570, Hebrew in 1580, and Greek in 1597. During the early years of the following century, the catechism was translated into Polish, Lithuanian, Italian, Bohemian, and Romanian. The Dutch East India and West India Companies were zealous promoters of the Heidelberg Catechism. Circling the globe with it, they sponsored translations into Malay (1623), Javanese (1623), Spanish (1628), Portuguese (1665), Singhalese (1726), and Tamil (1754). Eventually it was translated into such languages as Amharic, Sangiri, Arabic, Persian (Farsi), Chinese, and Japanese. Today it continues be disseminated around the globe in many other languages.

Criticism and Defense

The appearance of this catechism aroused immediate opposition from the Roman Catholic Church and from Emperor Maximilian II. It particularly met with strong disapproval from the Lutherans, for lifting up a Reformed banner in the land of Luther was considered a betrayal of his name and memory.

Three years later at the Diet of Augsburg in 1566, Frederick III was charged with "innovations" and the use of a catechism not agreeing with the (Lutheran) Augsburg Confession. It was demanded of him that he change or disown the catechism, and if he refused to do so he would be excluded from the Peace of the Empire and suffer the consequences. Hearing this, Frederick withdrew from the room for a moment.

He soon returned with his son Casimir, who carried a Bible, and began humbly but firmly to make his defense, testifying:

> Your Imperial Majesty, I continue in the conviction which I made known to you before I came here in person, that in matters of faith and conscience I acknowledge only one Lord who is Lord of all lords, and King of all kings. That is why I say that this is not a matter of the flesh, but of man's soul and its salvation which I have received from my Lord and Savior, Jesus Christ. His truth I am duty bound to guard. As regards Calvinism, I can say with God and my Christian conscience as witnesses that I have not read the books of Calvin, so that I can little say what is meant by Calvinism. But what my catechism teaches this I profess. This catechism has on its pages such abundant proof from Holy Scripture that it will remain unrefuted by men and will also remain my irrefutable belief. As regards the Augsburg Confession, your majesty knows that I signed it in good faith at Naumberg, and I continue to be true to that signature. For the rest, I comfort myself in this, that my Lord and Savior, Jesus Christ, has promised me and all His believers that whatever we lose for His name's sake here on earth shall be restored to us a hundredfold in the life to come. And with this I submit myself to the gracious consideration of your Imperial Majesty.

The Lord honored Frederick's bold defense of the faith and gave him the victory. Disagreeing with the judgment of the Emperor, the Diet voted that the Elector of the Palatinate was to be treated as belonging to the Alliance of Augsburg and within the jurisdiction of the Peace of the Empire.

English Versions

The Heidelberg Catechism was received by the English Church in the sixteenth century as an expression of her faith. Early translations were made by Turner (1567) and Parry (1591), but these were based on the Latin and the Dutch editions, and their sentence construction often deviated from the original German.

In America, Rev. Archibald Laidlie (1727–1779), serving in the Dutch Reformed Church in New York City, provided a new English version in 1765 at the request of his consistory. It became the standard version which is the basis of most older American editions. It was also used by the Reformed Church in the U.S. for many years.

In 1859 the General Synod of the Reformed Church in the U.S. appointed a committee to prepare a critical standard edition of the Catechism. This was issued in 1863, giving a historical and theological review of the catechism and the text in parallel columns in the original German, the Latin, modern German, and an English translation conforming closely to the original German. It became known as the *Tercentenary Edition.*

In evaluating this translation, Dr. James I. Good observed,

> The translation into English is carefully done from a literary standpoint, but it is somewhat marred by divergence from the original text, so as to favor the peculiar views of the Mercersburg Theology. ... This edition, however, was never officially adopted by the synod or the Church, and has come into only partial use in the Church, the older English translation of Laidlie being the one in common use. (*History of the Reformed Church in the U.S.* [New York, 1911], 405).

Since this time a number of modern translations have been made. Most of these have been sponsored by various Reformed and Presbyterian denominations.

Modern English Version

In the middle of the twentieth century, the continuing Reformed Church in the U.S. (Eureka Classis) prepared a revision of the *Tercentenary*, published in 1950. The Committee assigned to this task consulted two new critical German editions by August Lang and Wilhelm Niesel. Rev. Robert Grossmann writes that "this edition sought to return to the earliest text of the Catechism in German and to provide a most careful and direct translation of the same into English" (*You Shall Be My People* [1996], 107). It was first published with the German and English texts on opposite pages and was printed by Reliance Publishing Company. Later printings appeared only in English.

In the preface we read,

> Careful comparative studies of the original and the modern German versions, as also the Latin, the Dutch, and the English translations, were made, and, realizing that words and sentence construction become hallowed by use, alterations were made only with great caution after much deliberation to improve diction where permissible, or to state the intent of the original more accurately. The Tercentenary version of 1863 is followed closely.

In 1978 the text of the questions and answers was updated and later published by the 1986 Synod of the Reformed Church in the U.S. It retained the King James Version of the Scripture text. A minor revision of this version was made in 2011 under the direction of the 264th Synod, bringing the text of the Catechism into conformity with New King James Version usage. The present edition (2013) is now accompanied by the full Scripture reference text from the NKJV, to complete the updating of the Modern English Version. The ✢ symbol identifies additional Scripture references besides those found in the original text of the Catechism.

450th Anniversary Edition

Unique features in this special 450th Anniversary edition of the Catechism reflect the first edition published in 1563. A translation of Frederick III's original preface precedes the Catechism text. Afterwards, a series of Scripture quotations and the Apostles' Creed are provided in the order in which they appeared in the original edition. Two additional resources are given—an outline of the Catechism, and a harmony which cross-references similar topics in the Belgic Confession (1561) and Canons of Dort (1618–19).

The Heidelberg Catechism is a precious heritage of faith passed on to us from our Reformed fathers, as Rev. Paul Trieck writes,

> Countless people through the years have carried on the Heidelberg tradition. That is well, but will we and our children continue to carry on the Heidelberg's truths? Will we continue to commit it to our heads and our hearts? Will we faithfully teach our covenant children to walk in the doctrines it so clearly expounds? Would we be willing, as many before us, to put our life on the line to cling to the Christian faith as set forth in the Heidelberg? The use of the Heidelberg is very much a part of our past, but will we take that heritage with us into the future? To recount the rich heritage of our forefathers is an exercise in futility and no more than 'name-dropping' unless we still walk in those shoes and are committed to instill these truths in the hearts and minds of the generations to come. Just to preserve and honor a heritage as a thing of the past is to make an idolatrous icon of it. To persevere in the faith expressed in our Heidelberg heritage will be a blessing to us and to our covenant children. (*You Shall Be My People*, 1996, p. 209–10)

Faithful to the Word of God, the Catechism continues to supply believers with a trustworthy and eloquent statement of their faith. Now in its 450th year, the Heidelberg Catechism is being rediscovered as a fresh and contemporary means of articulating and transmitting the Reformed understanding of the Christian faith. May God continue to bless its use in His Church.

PREFACE, 1563

℘

WE, FREDERICK, by the grace of God, Elector Palatine on the Rhine, Archcarver and Elector of the Holy Roman Empire, Duke in Bavaria, etc., present to all and each of our Superintendents, Pastors, Preachers, Officers of the Church, and Schoolmasters throughout our Electorate of the Rhenish Palatinate, our grace and greeting, and do enjoin you to hereby know:

Inasmuch as we acknowledge that we are bound by the admonition of the Divine word, and also by natural duty and relation, and, have finally determined to order and administer our office, calling, and government, not only for the promotion and maintenance of quiet and peaceable living, and for the support of an upright and virtuous walk and behavior among our subjects, but also and above all, constantly to admonish and lead them to devout knowledge and fear of the Almighty and His holy word of salvation as the only foundation of all virtue and obedience, and to spare no pains, so far as lies in us, with all sincerity to promote their temporal and eternal welfare, and to contribute to the defense and maintenance of the same.

And, although apprised on entering upon our government, how our dear cousins and predecessors, Counts Palatine, Electors, etc., of noble and blessed memory, have instituted and proposed diverse Christian and profitable measures and means for the furtherance of the glory of God and the upholding of civil discipline and order:

Notwithstanding, this purpose was not in every respect prosecuted with the appropriate zeal, and the expected and desired fruit did not accrue therefrom—we are now induced not only to renew the same, but also, as the exigencies of the times demand, to improve, reform, and further to establish them. Therefore we also have ascertained that by no means the least defect of our system is found in the fact that our blooming youth are disposed to be careless in respect to Christian doctrine, both in the schools and churches of our principality—some, indeed, being entirely without Christian instruction, others being unsystematically taught, without any established, certain, and clear catechism, but merely according to individual plan or judgment; from which, among other great defects, the consequence has ensued, that they have, in too many instances, grown up without the fear of God and the knowledge of His word, having enjoyed no profitable instruction, or otherwise have been perplexed with irrelevant and needless questions, and at times have been burdened with unsound doctrines.

And now, whereas both temporal and spiritual offices, government and family discipline, cannot otherwise be maintained—and in order that discipline and obedience to authority and other virtues may increase and be multiplied among subjects—it is essential that our youth be trained in early life, and above all, in the pure and consistent doctrine of the holy Gospel, and be well exercised in the proper and true knowledge of God.

Therefore, we have regarded it as a high obligation, and as the most important duty of our government, to give attention to this matter, to do away with this defect, and to introduce the needful improvements:

And accordingly, with the advice and cooperation of our entire theological faculty in this place, and of all Superintendents and distinguished servants of the Church, we have secured the preparation of a summary course of instruction or catechism of our Christian Religion, according to the word of God, in the German and Latin languages; in order that the youth in churches and schools may be piously instructed in such Christian doctrine and be thoroughly trained therein, but also that the Pastors and Schoolmasters themselves may be provided with a fixed form and model by which to regulate the instruction of youth, and not, at their option, adopt daily changes, or introduce erroneous doctrine:

We do herewith affectionately admonish and enjoin upon every one of you, that you do, for the honor of God and our subjects, and also for the sake of your own soul's profit and welfare, thankfully accept this proffered Catechism or course of instruction, and that you do diligently and faithfully represent and explain the same according to its true import, to the youth in our schools and churches, and also from the pulpit to the common people, that you teach, and act, and live in accordance with it, in the assured hope, that if our youth in early life are earnestly instructed and educated in the word of God, it will please Almighty God also to grant reformation of public and private morals, and temporal and eternal welfare. Desiring, as above said, that all this may be accomplished, we have made this provision.

GIVEN AT HEIDELBERG, TUESDAY, THE NINETEENTH OF JANUARY,
IN THE YEAR 1563 AFTER THE BIRTH OF CHRIST,
OUR DEAR LORD AND SAVIOR.

Psalm 23

ଛ

The LORD is my shepherd; I shall not want.

He makes me to lie down in green pastures;

He leads me beside the still waters.

He restores my soul;

He leads me in the paths of righteousness

For His name's sake.

Yea, though I walk through the valley
of the shadow of death,

I will fear no evil; for You are with me;

Your rod and Your staff, they comfort me.

You prepare a table before me in
the presence of my enemies;

You anoint my head with oil;

My cup runs over.

Surely goodness and mercy shall follow me

All the days of my life;

And I will dwell in the house of the LORD forever.

Heidelberg Catechism

Modern English Version

ಐ

Introduction

Lord's Day 1

1. What is your only comfort in life and in death?

That I, with body and soul, both in life and in death,[1] am not my own,[2] but belong to my faithful Savior Jesus Christ,[3] who with His precious blood[4] has fully satisfied for all my sins,[5] and redeemed me from all the power of the devil;[6] and so preserves me[7] that without the will of my Father in heaven not a hair can fall from my head;[8] indeed, that all things must work together for my salvation.[9] Wherefore, by His Holy Spirit, He also assures me of eternal life,[10] and makes me heartily willing and ready from now on to live unto Him.[11]

[1] **Rom. 14:7–8.** For none of us lives to himself, and no one dies to himself. For if we live, we live to the Lord; and if we die, we die to the Lord. Therefore, whether we live or die, we are the Lord's.

[2] **1 Cor. 6:19.** Or do you not know that your body is the temple of the Holy Spirit who is in you, whom you have from God, and you are not your own?

[3] **1 Cor. 3:23.** And you are Christ's, and Christ is God's.

[4] **1 Pet. 1:18–19.** Knowing that you were not redeemed with corruptible things, like silver or gold, from your aimless conduct received by tradition from your fathers, but with the precious blood of Christ, as of a lamb without blemish and without spot.

[5] **1 Jn. 1:7.** But if we walk in the light as He is in the light, we have fellowship with one another, and the blood of Jesus Christ His Son cleanses us from all sin.

1 Jn. 2:2. And He Himself is the propitiation for our sins, and not for ours only but also for the whole world.

[6] **1 Jn. 3:8.** He who sins is of the devil, for the devil has sinned from the beginning. For this purpose the Son of God was manifested, that He might destroy the works of the devil.

[7] **Jn. 6:39.** This is the will of the Father who sent Me, that of all He has given Me I should lose nothing, but should raise it up at the last day.

[8] **Matt. 10:29–30.** Are not two sparrows sold for a copper coin? And not one of them falls to the ground apart from your Father's will. But the very hairs of your head are all numbered. Do not fear therefore; you are of more value than many sparrows.

    Lk. 21:18. But not a hair of your head shall be lost.

[9] **Rom. 8:28.** And we know that all things work together for good to those who love God, to those who are the called according to His purpose.

[10] **2 Cor. 1:21–22.** Now He who establishes us with you in Christ and has anointed us is God, who also has sealed us and given us the Spirit in our hearts as a guarantee.

    Eph. 1:13–14. In Him you also trusted, after you heard the word of truth, the gospel of your salvation; in whom also, having believed, you were sealed with the Holy Spirit of promise, who is the guarantee of our inheritance until the redemption of the purchased possession, to the praise of His glory.

    Rom. 8:16. The Spirit Himself bears witness with our spirit that we are children of God.

[11] **Rom. 8:1.** There is therefore now no condemnation to those who are in Christ Jesus, who do not walk according to the flesh, but according to the Spirit.

2. How many things are necessary for you to know, that in this comfort you may live and die happily?

Three things:[1] *First,* the greatness of my sin and misery.[2] *Second,* how I am redeemed from all my sins and misery.[3] *Third,* how I am to be thankful to God for such redemption.[4]

[1] **Lk. 24:46–47.** Then He said to them, "Thus it is written, and thus it was necessary for the Christ to suffer and to rise from the dead the third day, and that repentance and remission of sins should be preached in His name to all nations, beginning at Jerusalem."

    1 Cor. 6:11. And such were some of you. But you were washed, but you were sanctified, but you were justified in the name of the Lord Jesus and by the Spirit of our God.

Tit. 3:3–7. For we ourselves were also once foolish, disobedient, deceived, serving various lusts and pleasures, living in malice and envy, hateful and hating one another. But when the kindness and the love of God our Savior toward man appeared, not by works of righteousness which we have done, but according to His mercy He saved us, through the washing of regeneration and renewing of the Holy Spirit, whom He poured out on us abundantly through Jesus Christ our Savior, that having been justified by His grace we should become heirs according to the hope of eternal life.

[2] **Jn. 9:41.** Jesus said to them, "If you were blind, you would have no sin; but now you say, 'We see.' Therefore your sin remains."

Jn. 15:22. If I had not come and spoken to them, they would have no sin, but now they have no excuse for their sin.

[3] **Jn. 17:3.** And this is eternal life, that they may know You, the only true God, and Jesus Christ whom You have sent.

[4] **Eph. 5:8–11.** For you were once darkness, but now you are light in the Lord. Walk as children of light (for the fruit of the Spirit is in all goodness, righteousness, and truth), finding out what is acceptable to the Lord. And have no fellowship with the unfruitful works of darkness, but rather expose them.

1 Pet. 2:9–12. But you are a chosen generation, a royal priesthood, a holy nation, His own special people, that you may proclaim the praises of Him who called you out of darkness into His marvelous light; who once were not a people but are now the people of God, who had not obtained mercy but now have obtained mercy. Beloved, I beg you as sojourners and pilgrims, abstain from fleshly lusts which war against the soul, having your conduct honorable among the Gentiles, that when they speak against you as evildoers, they may, by your good works which they observe, glorify God in the day of visitation.

Rom. 6:11–14. Likewise you also, reckon yourselves to be dead indeed to sin, but alive to God in Christ Jesus our Lord. Therefore do not let sin reign in your mortal body, that you should obey it in its lusts. And do not present your members as instruments of unrighteousness to sin, but present yourselves to God as being alive from the dead, and your members as instruments of righteousness to God. For sin shall not have dominion over you, for you are not under law but under grace.

✠ **Rom. 7:24–25.** O wretched man that I am! Who will deliver me from this body of death? I thank God—through Jesus Christ our Lord! So then, with the mind I myself serve the law of God, but with the flesh the law of sin.

✠ **Gal. 3:13.** Christ has redeemed us from the curse of the law, having become a curse for us (for it is written, "Cursed is everyone who hangs on a tree").

✠ **Col. 3:17.** And whatever you do in word or deed, do all in the name of the Lord Jesus, giving thanks to God the Father through Him.

First Part: Our Misery

Lord's Day 2

3. From where do you know your misery?

From the Law of God.[1]

[1] **Rom. 3:20.** Therefore by the deeds of the law no flesh will be justified in His sight, for by the law is the knowledge of sin.

✢ **Rom. 7:7.** What shall we say then? Is the law sin? Certainly not! On the contrary, I would not have known sin except through the law. For I would not have known covetousness unless the law had said, "You shall not covet."

4. What does the Law of God require of us?

Christ teaches us in sum, Matthew 22,[1] *"You shall love the Lord your God with all your heart, with all your soul, and with all your mind. This is the first and great commandment. And the second is like it: You shall love your neighbor as yourself. On these two commandments hang all the Law and the Prophets."* (Matt. 22:37–40)

[1] **Lk. 10:27.** So He answered and said, "You shall love the Lord your God with all your heart, with all your soul, with all your strength, and with all your mind, and your neighbor as yourself."

✢ **Deut. 6:5.** You shall love the Lord your God with all your heart, with all your soul, and with all your strength.

✢ **Gal. 5:14.** For all the law is fulfilled in one word, even in this: "You shall love your neighbor as yourself."

5. Can you keep all this perfectly?

No,[1] for I am prone by nature to hate God and my neighbor.[2]

[1] **Rom. 3:10–12, 23.** As it is written: "There is none righteous, no, not one; there is none who understands; there is none who seeks after God. They have all turned aside; they have together become unprofitable; there is none who does good, no, not one." ... For all have sinned and fall short of the glory of God.

1 Jn. 1:8, 10. If we say that we have no sin, we deceive ourselves, and the truth is not in us. ... If we say that we have not sinned, we make Him a liar, and His word is not in us.

[2] Rom. 8:7. Because the carnal mind is enmity against God; for it is not subject to the law of God, nor indeed can be.

Eph. 2:3. Among whom also we all once conducted ourselves in the lusts of our flesh, fulfilling the desires of the flesh and of the mind, and were by nature children of wrath, just as the others.

Lord's Day 3

6. Did God create man thus, wicked and perverse?

No,[1] but God created man good and after His own image,[2] that is, in righteousness and true holiness, that he might rightly know God his Creator, heartily love Him, and live with Him in eternal blessedness, to praise and glorify Him.[3]

[1] Gen. 1:31. Then God saw everything that He had made, and indeed it was very good. So the evening and the morning were the sixth day.

[2] Gen. 1:26–27. Then God said, "Let Us make man in Our image, according to Our likeness; let them have dominion over the fish of the sea, over the birds of the air, and over the cattle, over all the earth and over every creeping thing that creeps on the earth." So God created man in His own image; in the image of God He created him; male and female He created them.

[3] 2 Cor. 3:18. But we all, with unveiled face, beholding as in a mirror the glory of the Lord, are being transformed into the same image from glory to glory, just as by the Spirit of the Lord.

Col. 3:10. And have put on the new man who is renewed in knowledge according to the image of Him who created him.

Eph. 4:24. And that you put on the new man which was created according to God, in true righteousness and holiness.

7. From where, then, does this depraved nature of man come?

From the fall and disobedience of our first parents, Adam and Eve, in Paradise,[1] whereby our nature became so corrupt that we are all conceived and born in sin.[2]

[1] **Gen. 3** (The whole chapter).

Rom. 5:12, 18–19. Therefore, just as through one man sin entered the world, and death through sin, and thus death spread to all men, because all sinned. ... Therefore, as through one man's offense judgment came to all men, resulting in condemnation, even so through one Man's righteous act the free gift came to all men, resulting in justification of life. For as by one man's disobedience many were made sinners, so also by one Man's obedience many will be made righteous.

[2] **Ps. 51:5.** Behold, I was brought forth in iniquity, and in sin my mother conceived me.

✢ **Ps. 14:2–3.** The LORD looks down from heaven upon the children of men, to see if there are any who understand, who seek God. They have all turned aside, they have together become corrupt; there is none who does good, no, not one.

8. But are we so depraved that we are completely incapable of any good and prone to all evil?

Yes,[1] unless we are born again by the Spirit of God.[2]

[1] **Jn. 3:6.** That which is born of the flesh is flesh, and that which is born of the Spirit is spirit.

Gen. 6:5. Then the LORD saw that the wickedness of man was great in the earth, and that every intent of the thoughts of his heart was only evil continually.

Job 14:4. Who can bring a clean thing out of an unclean? No one!

Isa. 53:6. All we like sheep have gone astray; we have turned, every one, to his own way; and the LORD has laid on Him the iniquity of us all.

[2] **Jn. 3:5.** Jesus answered, "Most assuredly, I say to you, unless one is born of water and the Spirit, he cannot enter the kingdom of God."

✢ **Gen. 8:21.** And the LORD smelled a soothing aroma. Then the LORD said in His heart, "I will never again curse the ground for man's sake, although the imagination of man's heart is evil from his youth; nor will I again destroy every living thing as I have done."

✢ **2 Cor. 3:5.** Not that we are sufficient of ourselves to think of anything as being from ourselves, but our sufficiency is from God.

✢ **Rom. 7:18.** For I know that in me (that is, in my flesh) nothing good dwells; for to will is present with me, but how to perform what is good I do not find.

✠ **Jer. 17:9.** The heart is deceitful above all things, and desperately wicked; who can know it?

Lord's Day 4

9. Does not God, then, do injustice to man by requiring of him in His Law that which he cannot perform?

No, for God so made man that he could perform it;[1] but man, through the instigation of the devil, by willful disobedience deprived himself and all his descendants of those divine gifts.[2]

[1] **Eph. 4:24.** And that you put on the new man which was created according to God, in true righteousness and holiness.

[2] **Rom. 5:12.** Therefore, just as through one man sin entered the world, and death through sin, and thus death spread to all men, because all sinned.

10. Will God allow such disobedience and apostasy to go unpunished?

Certainly not,[1] but He is terribly displeased with our inborn as well as our actual sins, and will punish them in just judgment in time and eternity, as He has declared, *"Cursed is everyone who does not continue in all things which are written in the book of the law, to do them."*

[1] **Heb. 9:27.** And as it is appointed for men to die once, but after this the judgment.

[2] **Deut. 27:26.** Cursed is the one who does not confirm all the words of this law. And all the people shall say, "Amen!"

> **Gal. 3:10.** For as many as are of the works of the law are under the curse; for it is written, "Cursed is everyone who does not continue in all things which are written in the book of the law, to do them."

✠ **Rom. 1:18.** For the wrath of God is revealed from heaven against all ungodliness and unrighteousness of men, who suppress the truth in unrighteousness.

✠ **Matt. 25:41.** Then He will also say to those on the left hand, "Depart from Me, you cursed, into the everlasting fire prepared for the devil and his angels."

11. But is not God also merciful?

God is indeed merciful,[1] but He is likewise just;[2] His justice therefore requires that sin which is committed against the most high majesty of God, be punished with extreme, that is, with everlasting punishment both of body and soul.

[1] **Ex. 34:6–7.** And the LORD passed before him and proclaimed, "The LORD, the LORD God, merciful and gracious, longsuffering, and abounding in goodness and truth, keeping mercy for thousands, forgiving iniquity and transgression and sin, by no means clearing the guilty, visiting the iniquity of the fathers upon the children and the children's children to the third and the fourth generation."

[2] **Ex. 20:5.** You shall not bow down to them nor serve them. For I, the LORD your God, am a jealous God, visiting the iniquity of the fathers upon the children to the third and fourth generations of those who hate Me.

Ps. 5:5–6. The boastful shall not stand in Your sight; You hate all workers of iniquity. You shall destroy those who speak falsehood; the LORD abhors the bloodthirsty and deceitful man.

2 Cor. 6:14–16. Do not be unequally yoked together with unbelievers. For what fellowship has righteousness with lawlessness? And what communion has light with darkness? And what accord has Christ with Belial? Or what part has a believer with an unbeliever? And what agreement has the temple of God with idols? For you are the temple of the living God. As God has said: "I will dwell in them and walk among them. I will be their God, and they shall be My people."

✠ **Rev. 14:11.** And the smoke of their torment ascends forever and ever; and they have no rest day or night, who worship the beast and his image, and whoever receives the mark of his name.

Second Part: Our Redemption

LORD'S DAY 5

12. Since, then, by the righteous judgment of God we deserve temporal and eternal punishment, how may we escape this punishment and be again received into favor?

God wills that His justice be satisfied;[1] therefore, we must make full satisfaction to that justice, either by ourselves or by another.[2]

[1] **Ex. 20:5.** You shall not bow down to them nor serve them. For I, the LORD your God, am a jealous God, visiting the iniquity of the fathers upon the children to the third and fourth generations of those who hate Me.

Ex. 23:7. Keep yourself far from a false matter; do not kill the innocent and righteous. For I will not justify the wicked.

[2] **Rom. 8:3–4.** For what the law could not do in that it was weak through the flesh, God did by sending His own Son in the likeness of sinful flesh, on account of sin: He condemned sin in the flesh, that the righteous requirement of the law might be fulfilled in us who do not walk according to the flesh but according to the Spirit.

13. Can we ourselves make this satisfaction?

Certainly not; on the contrary, we daily increase our guilt.[1]

[1] **Job 9:2–3.** Truly I know it is so, but how can a man be righteous before God? If one wished to contend with Him, he could not answer Him one time out of a thousand.

Job 15:15–16. If God puts no trust in His saints, and the heavens are not pure in His sight, How much less man, who is abominable and filthy, who drinks iniquity like water!

Matt. 6:12. And forgive us our debts, as we forgive our debtors.

✢ **Matt. 16:26.** For what profit is it to a man if he gains the whole world, and loses his own soul? Or what will a man give in exchange for his soul?

14. Can any mere creature make satisfaction for us?

None; for *first,* God will not punish any other creature for the sin which man committed;[1] and *further,* no mere creature can sustain the burden of God's eternal wrath against sin[2] and redeem others from it.

[1] **Heb. 2:14–18.** Inasmuch then as the children have partaken of flesh and blood, He Himself likewise shared in the same, that through death He might destroy him who had the power of death, that is, the devil, and release those who through fear of death were all their lifetime subject to bondage. For indeed He does not give aid to angels, but He does give aid to the seed of Abraham. Therefore, in all things He had to be made like His brethren,

that He might be a merciful and faithful High Priest in things pertaining to God, to make propitiation for the sins of the people. For in that He Himself has suffered, being tempted, He is able to aid those who are tempted.

[2] **Ps. 130:3.** If You, LORD, should mark iniquities, O Lord, who could stand?

15. What kind of mediator and redeemer, then, must we seek?

One who is a true[1] and righteous man,[2] and yet more powerful than all creatures, that is, one who is also true God.[3]

[1] **1 Cor. 15:21–22, 25–26.** For since by man came death, by Man also came the resurrection of the dead. For as in Adam all die, even so in Christ all shall be made alive. ... For He must reign till He has put all enemies under His feet. The last enemy that will be destroyed is death.

[2] **Jer. 33:16.** In those days Judah will be saved, and Jerusalem will dwell safely. And this is the name by which she will be called: THE LORD OUR RIGHTEOUSNESS.

Isa. 53:11. He shall see the labor of His soul, and be satisfied. By His knowledge My righteous Servant shall justify many, for He shall bear their iniquities.

2 Cor. 5:21. For He made Him who knew no sin to be sin for us, that we might become the righteousness of God in Him.

Heb. 7:15–16. And it is yet far more evident if, in the likeness of Melchizedek, there arises another priest who has come, not according to the law of a fleshly commandment, but according to the power of an endless life.

[3] **Isa. 7:14.** Therefore the Lord Himself will give you a sign: Behold, the virgin shall conceive and bear a Son, and shall call His name Immanuel.

Heb. 7:26. For such a High Priest was fitting for us, who is holy, harmless, undefiled, separate from sinners, and has become higher than the heavens.

LORD'S DAY 6

16. Why must He be a true and righteous man?

Because the justice of God requires[1] that the same human nature which has sinned should make satisfaction for sin; but one who is himself a sinner cannot satisfy for others.[2]

[1] **Rom: 5:15.** But the free gift is not like the offense. For if by the one man's offense many died, much more the grace of God and the gift by the grace of the one Man, Jesus Christ, abounded to many.

[2] **Isa. 53:3–5.** He is despised and rejected by men, a Man of sorrows and acquainted with grief. And we hid, as it were, our faces from Him; He was despised, and we did not esteem Him. Surely He has borne our griefs and carried our sorrows; yet we esteemed Him stricken, smitten by God, and afflicted. But He was wounded for our transgressions, He was bruised for our iniquities; the chastisement for our peace was upon Him, and by His stripes we are healed.

17. Why must He also be true God?

That by the power of His Godhead He might bear in His manhood the burden of God's wrath,[1] and so obtain for[2] and restore to us righteousness and life.[3]

[1] **Isa. 53:8.** He was taken from prison and from judgment, And who will declare His generation? For He was cut off from the land of the living; for the transgressions of My people He was stricken.

Acts 2:24. Whom God raised up, having loosed the pains of death, because it was not possible that He should be held by it.

[2] **Jn. 3:16.** For God so loved the world that He gave His only begotten Son, that whoever believes in Him should not perish but have everlasting life.

Acts 20:28. Therefore take heed to yourselves and to all the flock, among which the Holy Spirit has made you overseers, to shepherd the church of God which He purchased with His own blood.

[3] **1 Jn. 1:2.** The life was manifested, and we have seen, and bear witness, and declare to you that eternal life which was with the Father and was manifested to us.

18. But who now is that Mediator, who in one person is true God and also a true and righteous man?

Our Lord Jesus Christ,[1] who is freely given unto us for complete redemption and righteousness.[2]

[1] **Matt. 1:23.** Behold, the virgin shall be with child, and bear a Son, and they shall call His name Immanuel, which is translated, "God with us."

1 Tim. 3:16. And without controversy great is the mystery of Godliness: God was manifested in the flesh, justified in the Spirit, seen by angels, preached among the Gentiles, believed on in the world, received up in glory.

Lk. 2:11. For there is born to you this day in the city of David a Savior, who is Christ the Lord.

[2] **1 Cor. 1:30.** But of Him you are in Christ Jesus, who became for us wisdom from God—and righteousness and sanctification and redemption.

✛ **Acts 4:12.** Nor is there salvation in any other, for there is no other name under heaven given among men by which we must be saved.

19. From where do you know this?

From the Holy Gospel, which God Himself first revealed in Paradise,[1] afterwards proclaimed by the holy patriarchs[2] and prophets, and foreshadowed by the sacrifices and other ceremonies of the law,[3] and finally fulfilled by His well-beloved Son.[4]

[1] **Gen. 3:15.** And I will put enmity between you and the woman, and between your seed and her Seed; He shall bruise your head, and you shall bruise His heel.

[2] **Gen. 22:18.** In your seed all the nations of the earth shall be blessed, because you have obeyed My voice.

Gen. 49:10–11. The scepter shall not depart from Judah, nor a lawgiver from between his feet, until Shiloh comes; and to Him shall be the obedience of the people. Binding his donkey to the vine, and his donkey's colt to the choice vine, He washed his garments in wine, and his clothes in the blood of grapes.

Rom. 1:2. Which He promised before through His prophets in the Holy Scriptures.

Heb. 1:1. God, who at various times and in various ways spoke in time past to the fathers by the prophets.

Acts 3:22–24. For Moses truly said to the fathers, "The LORD your God will raise up for you a Prophet like me from your brethren. Him you shall hear in all things, whatever He says to you. And it shall be that every soul who will not hear that Prophet shall be utterly destroyed from among the people." Yes, and all the prophets, from Samuel and those who follow, as many as have spoken, have also foretold these days.

Acts 10:43. To Him all the prophets witness that, through His name, whoever believes in Him will receive remission of sins.

[3] **Jn. 5:46.** For if you believed Moses, you would believe Me; for he wrote about Me.

Heb. 10:7. Then I said, "Behold, I have come—in the volume of the book it is written of Me—to do Your will, O God."

[4] **Rom. 10:4.** For Christ is the end of the law for righteousness to everyone who believes.

Gal. 4:4–5. But when the fullness of the time had come, God sent forth His Son, born of a woman, born under the law, to redeem those who were under the law, that we might receive the adoption as sons.

✢ **Heb. 10:1.** For the law, having a shadow of the good things to come, and not the very image of the things, can never with these same sacrifices, which they offer continually year by year, make those who approach perfect.

LORD'S DAY 7

20. Are all men, then, saved by Christ as they have perished in Adam?

No, only those who by true faith are ingrafted into Him and receive all His benefits.[1]

[1] **Jn. 1:12–13.** But as many as received Him, to them He gave the right to become children of God, to those who believe in His name: who were born, not of blood, nor of the will of the flesh, nor of the will of man, but of God.

1 Cor. 15:22. For as in Adam all die, even so in Christ all shall be made alive.

Ps. 2:12. Kiss the Son, lest He be angry, and you perish in the way, when His wrath is kindled but a little. Blessed are all those who put their trust in Him.

Rom. 11:20. Well said. Because of unbelief they were broken off, and you stand by faith. Do not be haughty, but fear.

Heb. 4:2–3. For indeed the gospel was preached to us as well as to them; but the word which they heard did not profit them, not being mixed with faith in those who heard it. For we who have believed do enter that rest, as He has said: "So I swore in My wrath, 'They shall not enter My rest,'" although the works were finished from the foundation of the world.

Heb. 10:39. But we are not of those who draw back to perdition, but of those who believe to the saving of the soul.

21. What is true faith?

True faith is not only a sure knowledge, whereby I hold for truth all that God has revealed to us in His Word,[1] but also a hearty trust,[2] which the Holy Spirit[3] works in me by the Gospel,[4] that not only to others, but to me also, forgiveness of sins, everlasting righteousness, and salvation are freely given by God,[5] merely of grace, only for the sake of Christ's merits.[6]

[1] **Jas. 1:6.** But let him ask in faith, with no doubting, for he who doubts is like a wave of the sea driven and tossed by the wind.

[2] **Rom. 4:16–18.** Therefore it is of faith that it might be according to grace, so that the promise might be sure to all the seed, not only to those who are of the law, but also to those who are of the faith of Abraham, who is the father of us all (as it is written, "I have made you a father of many nations") in the presence of Him whom he believed—God, who gives life to the dead and calls those things which do not exist as though they did; who, contrary to hope, in hope believed, so that he became the father of many nations, according to what was spoken, "So shall your descendants be."

Rom. 5:1. Therefore, having been justified by faith, we have peace with God through our Lord Jesus Christ,

[3] **2 Cor. 4:13.** And since we have the same spirit of faith, according to what is written, "I believed and therefore I spoke," we also believe and therefore speak.

Phil. 1:19, 29. For I know that this will turn out for my deliverance through your prayer and the supply of the Spirit of Jesus Christ, ... For to you it has been granted on behalf of Christ, not only to believe in Him, but also to suffer for His sake.

[4] **Rom. 1:16.** For I am not ashamed of the gospel of Christ, for it is the power of God to salvation for everyone who believes, for the Jew first and also for the Greek.

Rom. 10:17. So then faith comes by hearing, and hearing by the word of God.

[5] **Heb. 11:1 2.** Now faith is the substance of things hoped for, the evidence of things not seen. For by it the elders obtained a good testimony.

Rom. 1:17. For in it the righteousness of God is revealed from faith to faith; as it is written, "The just shall live by faith."

[6] **Eph. 2:7–9.** That in the ages to come He might show the exceeding riches of His grace in His kindness toward us in Christ Jesus. For by grace you

have been saved through faith, and that not of yourselves; it is the gift of God, not of works, lest anyone should boast.

Rom. 3:24–25. Being justified freely by His grace through the redemption that is in Christ Jesus, whom God set forth as a propitiation by His blood, through faith, to demonstrate His righteousness, because in His forbearance God had passed over the sins that were previously committed.

Gal. 2:16. Knowing that a man is not justified by the works of the law but by faith in Jesus Christ, even we have believed in Christ Jesus, that we might be justified by faith in Christ and not by the works of the law; for by the works of the law no flesh shall be justified.

✢ **Acts 10:43.** To Him all the prophets witness that, through His name, whoever believes in Him will receive remission of sins.

22. What, then, is necessary for a Christian to believe?

All that is promised us in the Gospel,[1] which the articles of our catholic, undoubted Christian faith teach us in summary.

[1] **Jn. 20:31.** But these are written that you may believe that Jesus is the Christ, the Son of God, and that believing you may have life in His name.

Matt. 28:20. Teaching them to observe all things that I have commanded you; and lo, I am with you always, even to the end of the age. Amen.

✢ **2 Pet. 1:21.** For prophecy never came by the will of man, but holy men of God spoke as they were moved by the Holy Spirit.

✢ **2 Tim. 3:15.** And that from childhood you have known the Holy Scriptures, which are able to make you wise for salvation through faith which is in Christ Jesus.

23. What are these articles?

I believe in GOD THE FATHER Almighty, Maker of heaven and earth.

And in JESUS CHRIST, His only-begotten Son, our Lord: who was conceived by the Holy Spirit, born of the virgin Mary, suffered under Pontius Pilate, was crucified, dead, and buried; He descended into hell; the third day He rose from the dead; He ascended into heaven, and sits at the right hand of God the Father Almighty; from there He will come to judge the living and the dead.

I believe in the HOLY SPIRIT, the holy, catholic Church, the communion of saints, the forgiveness of sins, the resurrection of the body, and the life everlasting.

LORD'S DAY 8

24. How are these articles divided?

Into three parts: the first is of God the Father and our creation; the second, of God the Son and our redemption; the third, of God the Holy Spirit and our sanctification.[1]

[1] **1 Pet. 1:2.** Elect according to the foreknowledge of God the Father, in sanctification of the Spirit, for obedience and sprinkling of the blood of Jesus Christ: Grace to you and peace be multiplied.

✣ **1 Jn. 5:7.** For there are three that bear witness in heaven: the Father, the Word, and the Holy Spirit; and these three are one.

25. Since there is but one Divine Being,[1] why do you speak of three persons: Father, Son, and Holy Spirit?

Because God has so revealed Himself in His Word,[2] that these three distinct persons are the one, true, eternal God.

[1] **Deut. 6:4.** Hear, O Israel: The LORD our God, the LORD is one!

[2] **Isa. 61:1.** The Spirit of the Lord God is upon Me, because the LORD has anointed Me to preach good tidings to the poor; He has sent Me to heal the brokenhearted, to proclaim liberty to the captives, and the opening of the prison to those who are bound.

Ps. 110:1. The LORD said to my Lord, "Sit at My right hand, till I make Your enemies Your footstool."

Matt. 3:16–17. When He had been baptized, Jesus came up immediately from the water; and behold, the heavens were opened to Him, and He saw the Spirit of God descending like a dove and alighting upon Him. And suddenly a voice came from heaven, saying, "This is My beloved Son, in whom I am well pleased."

Matt. 28:19. Go therefore and make disciples of all the nations, baptizing them in the name of the Father and of the Son and of the Holy Spirit.

1 Jn. 5:7. For there are three that bear witness in heaven: the Father, the Word, and the Holy Spirit; and these three are one.

✢ 2 Cor. 13:14. The grace of the Lord Jesus Christ, and the love of God, and the communion of the Holy Spirit be with you all. Amen.

God the Father

LORD's DAY 9

26. What do you believe when you say, "I believe in God the Father Almighty, Maker of heaven and earth"?

That the eternal Father of our Lord Jesus Christ, who of nothing made heaven and earth with all that is in them,[1] who likewise upholds, and governs them by His eternal counsel and providence,[2] is for the sake of Christ, His Son, my God and my Father,[3] in whom I so trust as to have no doubt that He will provide me with all things necessary for body and soul;[4] and further, that whatever evil He sends upon me in this valley of tears, He will turn to my good;[5] for He is able to do it, being Almighty God,[6] and willing also, being a faithful Father.[7]

[1] **Gen. 1:31.** Then God saw everything that He had made, and indeed it was very good. So the evening and the morning were the sixth day.

Ps. 33:6. By the word of the LORD the heavens were made, and all the host of them by the breath of His mouth.

✢ **Col. 1:16.** For by Him all things were created that are in heaven and that are on earth, visible and invisible, whether thrones or dominions or principalities or powers. All things were created through Him and for Him.

✢ **Heb. 11:3.** By faith we understand that the worlds were framed by the word of God, so that the things which are seen were not made of things which are visible.

[2] **Ps. 104:2–5.** Who cover Yourself with light as with a garment, who stretch out the heavens like a curtain. He lays the beams of His upper chambers in the waters, who makes the clouds His chariot, who walks on the wings of the wind, who makes His angels spirits, His ministers a flame of fire. You who laid the foundations of the earth, so that it should not be moved forever.

Matt. 10:30. But the very hairs of your head are all numbered.

Heb. 1:3. Who being the brightness of His glory and the express image of His person, and upholding all things by the word of His power, when He had by Himself purged our sins, sat down at the right hand of the Majesty on high.

Ps. 115:3. But our God is in heaven; He does whatever He pleases.

✢ **Acts 17:24–25.** God, who made the world and everything in it, since He is Lord of heaven and earth, does not dwell in temples made with hands. Nor is He worshiped with men's hands, as though He needed anything, since He gives to all life, breath, and all things.

[3] **Jn. 1:12.** But as many as received Him, to them He gave the right to become children of God, to those who believe in His name.

Rom. 8:15. For you did not receive the spirit of bondage again to fear, but you received the Spirit of adoption by whom we cry out, "Abba, Father."

Gal. 4:5–7. To redeem those who were under the law, that we might receive the adoption as sons. And because you are sons, God has sent forth the Spirit of His Son into your hearts, crying out, "Abba, Father!" Therefore you are no longer a slave but a son, and if a son, then an heir of God through Christ.

Eph. 1:5. Having predestined us to adoption as sons by Jesus Christ to Himself, according to the good pleasure of His will.

✢ **Eph. 3:14–16.** For this reason I bow my knees to the Father of our Lord Jesus Christ, from whom the whole family in heaven and earth is named, that He would grant you, according to the riches of His glory, to be strengthened with might through His Spirit in the inner man.

✢ **Matt. 6:8.** Therefore do not be like them. For your Father knows the things you have need of before you ask Him.

[4] **Ps. 55:22.** Cast your burden on the LORD, and He shall sustain you; He shall never permit the righteous to be moved.

Matt. 6:25–26. Therefore I say to you, do not worry about your life, what you will eat or what you will drink; nor about your body, what you will put on. Is not life more than food and the body more than clothing? Look at the birds of the air, for they neither sow nor reap nor gather into barns; yet your heavenly Father feeds them. Are you not of more value than they? (See also Luke 12:22–24.)

Ps. 90:1–2. LORD, You have been our dwelling place in all generations. Before the mountains were brought forth, or ever You had formed the earth and the world, even from everlasting to everlasting, You are God.

[5] **Rom. 8:28.** And we know that all things work together for good to those who love God, to those who are the called according to His purpose.

✛ **Acts 17:27–28.** So that they should seek the Lord, in the hope that they might grope for Him and find Him, though He is not far from each one of us; for in Him we live and move and have our being, as also some of your own poets have said, "For we are also His offspring."

[6] **Rom. 10:12.** For there is no distinction between Jew and Greek, for the same Lord over all is rich to all who call upon Him.

[7] **Matt. 7:9–11.** Or what man is there among you who, if his son asks for bread, will give him a stone? Or if he asks for a fish, will he give him a serpent? If you then, being evil, know how to give good gifts to your children, how much more will your Father who is in heaven give good things to those who ask Him!

✛ **Num. 23:19.** God is not a man, that He should lie, nor a son of man, that He should repent. Has He said, and will He not do? Or has He spoken, and will He not make it good?

Lord's Day 10

27. What do you understand by the providence of God?

The almighty, everywhere-present power of God,[1] whereby, as it were by His hand, He still upholds heaven and earth with all creatures,[2] and so governs them that herbs and grass, rain and drought, fruitful and barren years, meat and drink,[3] health and sickness,[4] riches and poverty,[5] indeed, all things come not by chance, but by His fatherly hand.

[1] **Acts 17:25–26.** Nor is He worshiped with men's hands, as though He needed anything, since He gives to all life, breath, and all things. And He has made from one blood every nation of men to dwell on all the face of the earth, and has determined their preappointed times and the boundaries of their dwellings.

[2] **Heb. 1:3.** Who being the brightness of His glory and the express image of His person, and upholding all things by the word of His power, when He had by Himself purged our sins, sat down at the right hand of the Majesty on high.

[3] **Jer. 5:24.** They do not say in their heart, "Let us now fear the Lord our God, who gives rain, both the former and the latter, in its season. He reserves for us the appointed weeks of the harvest."

✛ **Acts 14:17.** Nevertheless He did not leave Himself without witness, in that He did good, gave us rain from heaven and fruitful seasons, filling our hearts with food and gladness.

[4] **Jn. 9:3.** Jesus answered, "Neither this man nor his parents sinned, but that the works of God should be revealed in him."

[5] **Prov. 22:2.** The rich and the poor have this in common, the LORD is the maker of them all.

✣ **Ps. 103:19.** The LORD has established His throne in heaven, and His kingdom rules over all.

✣ **Rom. 5:3–5a.** And not only that, but we also glory in tribulations, knowing that tribulation produces perseverance; and perseverance, character; and character, hope. Now hope does not disappoint, because the love of God has been poured out in our hearts by the Holy Spirit who was given to us.

28. What does it profit us to know that God created, and by His providence upholds, all things?

That we may be patient in adversity,[1] thankful in prosperity,[2] and for what is future have good confidence in our faithful God and Father, that no creature shall separate us from His love,[3] since all creatures are so in His hand, that without His will they cannot so much as move.[4]

[1] **Rom. 5:3.** And not only that, but we also glory in tribulations, knowing that tribulation produces perseverance.

Jas. 1:3. Knowing that the testing of your faith produces patience.

Job 1:21. And he said, "Naked I came from my mother's womb, and naked shall I return there. The LORD gave, and the LORD has taken away; blessed be the name of the LORD."

[2] **Deut. 8:10.** When you have eaten and are full, then you shall bless the LORD your God for the good land which He has given you.

1 Thess. 5:18. In everything give thanks; for this is the will of God in Christ Jesus for you.

[3] **Rom. 8:35, 38–39.** Who shall separate us from the love of Christ? Shall tribulation, or distress, or persecution, or famine, or nakedness, or peril, or sword? ... For I am persuaded that neither death nor life, nor angels nor principalities nor powers, nor things present nor things to come, nor height nor depth, nor any other created thing, shall be able to separate us from the love of God which is in Christ Jesus our Lord.

[4] **Job 1:12.** And the LORD said to Satan, "Behold, all that he has is in your power; only do not lay a hand on his person." So Satan went out from the presence of the LORD.

Acts 17:25–28. Nor is He worshiped with men's hands, as though He needed anything, since He gives to all life, breath, and all things. And He has made from one blood every nation of men to dwell on all the face of the earth, and has determined their preappointed times and the boundaries of their dwellings, so that they should seek the Lord, in the hope that they might grope for Him and find Him, though He is not far from each one of us; for in Him we live and move and have our being, as also some of your own poets have said, "For we are also His offspring."

Prov. 21:1. The king's heart is in the hand of the Lord, like the rivers of water; He turns it wherever He wishes.

✠ **Ps. 71:7.** I have become as a wonder to many, but You are my strong refuge.

✠ **2 Cor. 1:10.** Who delivered us from so great a death, and does deliver us; in whom we trust that He will still deliver us.

God the Son

Lord's Day 11

29. Why is the Son of God called "Jesus," that is, Savior?

Because He saves us from all our sins,[1] and because salvation is not to be sought or found in any other.[2]

[1] **Matt. 1:21.** And she will bring forth a Son, and you shall call His name Jesus, for He will save His people from their sins.

   Heb. 7:25. Therefore He is also able to save to the uttermost those who come to God through Him, since He always lives to make intercession for them.

[2] **Acts 4:12.** Nor is there salvation in any other, for there is no other name under heaven given among men by which we must be saved.

✠ **Lk. 2:10–11.** Then the angel said to them, "Do not be afraid, for behold, I bring you good tidings of great joy which will be to all people. For there is born to you this day in the city of David a Savior, who is Christ the Lord."

30. Do those also believe in the only Savior Jesus, who seek their salvation and welfare from "saints," themselves, or anywhere else?

No; although they make their boast of Him, yet in their deeds they deny the only Savior Jesus;[1] for either Jesus is not a complete Savior, or they who by true faith receive this Savior, must have in Him all that is necessary to their salvation.[2]

[1] **1 Cor. 1:13.** Is Christ divided? Was Paul crucified for you? Or were you baptized in the name of Paul?

1 Cor. 1:30–31. But of Him you are in Christ Jesus, who became for us wisdom from God—and righteousness and sanctification and redemption—that, as it is written, "He who glories, let him glory in the LORD."

Gal. 5:4. You have become estranged from Christ, you who attempt to be justified by law; you have fallen from grace.

[2] **Isa. 9:7.** Of the increase of His government and peace there will be no end, upon the throne of David and over His kingdom, to order it and establish it with judgment and justice from that time forward, even forever. The zeal of the LORD of hosts will perform this.

Col. 1:20. And by Him to reconcile all things to Himself, by Him, whether things on earth or things in heaven, having made peace through the blood of His cross.

Col. 2:10. And you are complete in Him, who is the head of all principality and power.

Jn. 1:16. And of His fullness we have all received, and grace for grace.

✢ **Matt. 23:28.** Even so you also outwardly appear righteous to men, but inside you are full of hypocrisy and lawlessness.

LORD'S DAY 12

31. Why is He called "Christ," that is, Anointed?

Because He is ordained of God the Father and anointed with the Holy Spirit[1] to be our chief Prophet and Teacher,[2] who has fully revealed to us the secret counsel and will of God concerning our redemption;[3] and our only High Priest,[4] who by the one sacrifice of His body, has redeemed us, and ever lives to make intercession for us with the Father;[5] and our eternal King, who governs us by His Word and Spirit, and defends and preserves us in the redemption obtained for us.[6]

[1] **Heb. 1:9.** You have loved righteousness and hated lawlessness; therefore God, Your God, has anointed You with the oil of gladness more than Your companions.

[2] **Deut. 18:15.** The LORD your God will raise up for you a Prophet like me from your midst, from your brethren. Him you shall hear.

Acts 3:22. For Moses truly said to the fathers, "The LORD your God will raise up for you a Prophet like me from your brethren. Him you shall hear in all things, whatever He says to you."

[3] **Jn. 1:18.** No one has seen God at any time. The only begotten Son, who is in the bosom of the Father, He has declared Him.

Jn. 15:15. No longer do I call you servants, for a servant does not know what his master is doing; but I have called you friends, for all things that I heard from My Father I have made known to you.

[4] **Ps. 110:4.** The LORD has sworn and will not relent, "You are a priest forever according to the order of Melchizedek."

Heb. 7:21. (For they have become priests without an oath, but He with an oath by Him who said to Him: "The LORD has sworn and will not relent, You are a priest forever according to the order of Melchizedek.")

[5] **Rom. 5:9–10.** Much more then, having now been justified by His blood, we shall be saved from wrath through Him. For if when we were enemies we were reconciled to God through the death of His Son, much more, having been reconciled, we shall be saved by His life.

[6] **Ps. 2:6.** Yet I have set My King on My holy hill of Zion.

Lk. 1:33. And He will reign over the house of Jacob forever, and of His kingdom there will be no end.

Matt. 28:18. And Jesus came and spoke to them, saying, "All authority has been given to Me in heaven and on earth."

✛ **Isa. 61:1–2.** The Spirit of the Lord GOD is upon Me, because the LORD has anointed Me to preach good tidings to the poor; He has sent Me to heal the brokenhearted, to proclaim liberty to the captives, and the opening of the prison to those who are bound; to proclaim the acceptable year of the LORD, and the day of vengeance of our God; to comfort all who mourn.

✛ **1 Pet. 2:24.** Who Himself bore our sins in His own body on the tree, that we, having died to sins, might live for righteousness—by whose stripes you were healed.

✛ **Rev. 19:16.** And He has on His robe and on His thigh a name written: KING OF KINGS AND LORD OF LORDS.

32. But why are you called a Christian?

Because by faith I am a member of Christ[1] and thus a partaker of His anointing,[2] in order that I also may confess His Name,[3] may present myself a living sacrifice of thankfulness to Him,[4] and with a free conscience may fight against sin and the devil in this life,[5] and hereafter in eternity reign with Him over all creatures.[6]

[1] **Acts 11:26.** And when he had found him, he brought him to Antioch. So it was that for a whole year they assembled with the church and taught a great many people. And the disciples were first called Christians in Antioch.

1 Jn. 2:27. But the anointing which you have received from Him abides in you, and you do not need that anyone teach you; but as the same anointing teaches you concerning all things, and is true, and is not a lie, and just as it has taught you, you will abide in Him.

✢ **1 Jn. 2:20.** But you have an anointing from the Holy One, and you know all things.

[2] **Acts 2:17.** "And it shall come to pass in the last days," says God, "that I will pour out of My Spirit on all flesh; your sons and your daughters shall prophesy, your young men shall see visions, your old men shall dream dreams."

[3] **Mk. 8:38.** For whoever is ashamed of Me and My words in this adulterous and sinful generation, of him the Son of Man also will be ashamed when He comes in the glory of His Father with the holy angels.

[4] **Rom. 12:1.** I beseech you therefore, brethren, by the mercies of God, that you present your bodies a living sacrifice, holy, acceptable to God, which is your reasonable service.

Rev. 5:8, 10. Now when He had taken the scroll, the four living creatures and the twenty-four elders fell down before the Lamb, each having a harp, and golden bowls full of incense, which are the prayers of the saints. ... And have made us kings and priests to our God; and we shall reign on the earth.

1 Pet. 2:9. But you are a chosen generation, a royal priesthood, a holy nation, His own special people, that you may proclaim the praises of Him who called you out of darkness into His marvelous light.

Rev. 1:6. And has made us kings and priests to His God and Father, to Him be glory and dominion forever and ever. Amen.

[5] **1 Tim. 1:18–19.** This charge I commit to you, son Timothy, according to the prophecies previously made concerning you, that by them you may wage the good warfare, having faith and a good conscience, which some having rejected, concerning the faith have suffered shipwreck.

[6] **2 Tim. 2:12.** If we endure, we shall also reign with Him. If we deny Him, He also will deny us.

✢ **Eph. 6:12.** For we do not wrestle against flesh and blood, but against principalities, against powers, against the rulers of the darkness of this age, against spiritual hosts of wickedness in the heavenly places.

✢ **Rev. 3:21.** To him who overcomes I will grant to sit with Me on My throne, as I also overcame and sat down with My Father on His throne.

Lord's Day 13

33. Why is He called God's "only begotten Son," since we also are the children of God?

Because Christ alone is the eternal, natural Son of God,[1] but we are children of God by adoption, through grace, for His sake.[2]

[1] **Jn. 1:14, 18.** And the Word became flesh and dwelt among us, and we beheld His glory, the glory as of the only begotten of the Father, full of grace and truth. ... No one has seen God at any time. The only begotten Son, who is in the bosom of the Father, He has declared Him.

[2] **Rom. 8:15–17.** For you did not receive the spirit of bondage again to fear, but you received the Spirit of adoption by whom we cry out, "Abba, Father." The Spirit Himself bears witness with our spirit that we are children of God, and if children, then heirs—heirs of God and joint heirs with Christ, if indeed we suffer with Him, that we may also be glorified together.

Eph. 1:5–6. Having predestined us to adoption as sons by Jesus Christ to Himself, according to the good pleasure of His will, to the praise of the glory of His grace, by which He made us accepted in the Beloved.

✢ **1 Jn. 3:1.** Behold what manner of love the Father has bestowed on us, that we should be called children of God! Therefore the world does not know us, because it did not know Him.

34. Why do you call Him "our Lord"?

Because not with silver or gold, but with His precious blood, He has redeemed and purchased us, body and soul, from sin and from all the power of the devil, to be His own.[1]

[1] **1 Pet. 1:18–19.** Knowing that you were not redeemed with corruptible things, like silver or gold, from your aimless conduct received by tradition

from your fathers, but with the precious blood of Christ, as of a lamb without blemish and without spot.

1 Pet. 2:9. But you are a chosen generation, a royal priesthood, a holy nation, His own special people, that you may proclaim the praises of Him who called you out of darkness into His marvelous light.

1 Cor. 6:20. For you were bought at a price; therefore glorify God in your body and in your spirit, which are God's.

1 Cor. 7:23. You were bought at a price; do not become slaves of men.

✣ **Acts 2:36.** Therefore let all the house of Israel know assuredly that God has made this Jesus, whom you crucified, both Lord and Christ.

✣ **Tit. 2:14.** Who gave Himself for us, that He might redeem us from every lawless deed and purify for Himself His own special people, zealous for good works.

✣ **Col. 1:14.** In whom we have redemption through His blood, the forgiveness of sins.

Lord's Day 14

35. What is the meaning of "conceived by the Holy Spirit, born of the virgin Mary"?

That the eternal Son of God, who is[1] and continues true and eternal God,[2] took upon Himself the very nature of man, of the flesh and blood of the virgin Mary,[3] by the operation of the Holy Spirit;[4] so that He might also be the true seed of David,[5] like unto His brethren in all things,[6] except for sin.[7]

[1] **Jn. 1:1.** In the beginning was the Word, and the Word was with God, and the Word was God.

Rom. 1:3–4. Concerning His Son Jesus Christ our Lord, who was born of the seed of David according to the flesh, and declared to be the Son of God with power according to the Spirit of holiness, by the resurrection from the dead.

[2] **Rom. 9:5.** Of whom are the fathers and from whom, according to the flesh, Christ came, who is over all, the eternally blessed God. Amen.

[3] **Gal. 4:4.** But when the fullness of the time had come, God sent forth His Son, born of a woman, born under the law.

Jn. 1:14. And the Word became flesh and dwelt among us, and we beheld His glory, the glory as of the only begotten of the Father, full of grace and truth.

[4] **Matt. 1:18–20.** Now the birth of Jesus Christ was as follows: After His mother Mary was betrothed to Joseph, before they came together, she was found with child of the Holy Spirit. Then Joseph her husband, being a just man, and not wanting to make her a public example, was minded to put her away secretly. But while he thought about these things, behold, an angel of the Lord appeared to him in a dream, saying, "Joseph, son of David, do not be afraid to take to you Mary your wife, for that which is conceived in her is of the Holy Spirit."

Lk. 1:35. And the angel answered and said to her, "The Holy Spirit will come upon you, and the power of the Highest will overshadow you; therefore, also, that Holy One who is to be born will be called the Son of God."

[5] **Ps. 132:11.** The Lord has sworn in truth to David; He will not turn from it: "I will set upon your throne the fruit of your body."

[6] **Phil. 2:7.** But made Himself of no reputation, taking the form of a bond-servant, and coming in the likeness of men.

[7] **Heb. 4:15.** For we do not have a High Priest who cannot sympathize with our weaknesses, but was in all points tempted as we are, yet without sin.

✢ **1 Jn. 5:20.** And we know that the Son of God has come and has given us an understanding, that we may know Him who is true; and we are in Him who is true, in His Son Jesus Christ. This is the true God and eternal life.

36. What benefit do you receive from the holy conception and birth of Christ?

That He is our Mediator,[1] and with His innocence and perfect holiness covers, in the sight of God, my sin, wherein I was conceived.[2]

[1] **Heb. 2:16–17.** For indeed He does not give aid to angels, but He does give aid to the seed of Abraham. Therefore, in all things He had to be made like His brethren, that He might be a merciful and faithful High Priest in things pertaining to God, to make propitiation for the sins of the people.

[2] **Ps. 32:1.** Blessed is he whose transgression is forgiven, whose sin is covered.

✢ **1 Jn. 1:9.** If we confess our sins, He is faithful and just to forgive us our sins and to cleanse us from all unrighteousness.

LORD'S DAY 15

37. What do you understand by the word "suffered"?

That all the time He lived on earth, but especially at the end of His life, He bore, in body and soul, the wrath of God against the sin of the whole human race;[1] in order that by His suffering, as the only atoning sacrifice,[2] He might redeem our body and soul from everlasting damnation, and obtain for us the grace of God, righteousness, and eternal life.

[1] **1 Pet. 2:24.** Who Himself bore our sins in His own body on the tree, that we, having died to sins, might live for righteousness—by whose stripes you were healed.

Isa. 53:12. Therefore I will divide Him a portion with the great, and He shall divide the spoil with the strong, because He poured out His soul unto death, and He was numbered with the transgressors, and He bore the sin of many, and made intercession for the transgressors.

[2] **1 Jn. 2:2.** And He Himself is the propitiation for our sins, and not for ours only but also for the whole world.

1 Jn. 4:10. In this is love, not that we loved God, but that He loved us and sent His Son to be the propitiation for our sins.

Rom. 3:25–26. Whom God set forth as a propitiation by His blood, through faith, to demonstrate His righteousness, because in His forbearance God had passed over the sins that were previously committed, to demonstrate at the present time His righteousness, that He might be just and the justifier of the one who has faith in Jesus.

✤ **Ps. 22:14–16.** I am poured out like water, and all My bones are out of joint; My heart is like wax; it has melted within Me. My strength is dried up like a potsherd, and My tongue clings to My jaws; You have brought Me to the dust of death. For dogs have surrounded Me; the congregation of the wicked has enclosed Me. They pierced My hands and My feet.

✤ **Matt. 26:38.** Then He said to them, "My soul is exceedingly sorrowful, even to death. Stay here and watch with Me."

✤ **Rom. 5:6.** For when we were still without strength, in due time Christ died for the ungodly.

38. Why did He suffer "under Pontius Pilate" as judge?

That He, being innocent, might be condemned by the temporal judge,[1] and thereby deliver us from the severe judgment of God, to which we were exposed.[2]

[1] **Acts 4:27–28.** For truly against Your holy Servant Jesus, whom You anointed, both Herod and Pontius Pilate, with the Gentiles and the people of Israel, were gathered together to do whatever Your hand and Your purpose determined before to be done.

Lk. 23:13–15. Then Pilate, when he had called together the chief priests, the rulers, and the people, said to them, "You have brought this Man to me, as one who misleads the people. And indeed, having examined Him in your presence, I have found no fault in this Man concerning those things of which you accuse Him; no, neither did Herod, for I sent you back to him; and indeed nothing deserving of death has been done by Him."

Jn. 19:4. Pilate then went out again, and said to them, "Behold, I am bringing Him out to you, that you may know that I find no fault in Him."

[2] **Ps. 69:4.** Those who hate me without a cause are more than the hairs of my head; they are mighty who would destroy me, being my enemies wrongfully; though I have stolen nothing, I still must restore it.

2 Cor. 5:21. For He made Him who knew no sin to be sin for us, that we might become the righteousness of God in Him.

✢ **Matt. 27:24.** When Pilate saw that he could not prevail at all, but rather that a tumult was rising, he took water and washed his hands before the multitude, saying, "I am innocent of the blood of this just Person. You see to it."

39. Is there anything more in His having been "crucified" than if He had suffered some other death?

Yes, for thereby I am assured that He took upon Himself the curse which lay upon me,[1] because the death of the cross was accursed of God.[2]

[1] **Gal. 3:13–14.** Christ has redeemed us from the curse of the law, having become a curse for us (for it is written, "Cursed is everyone who hangs on a tree"), that the blessing of Abraham might come upon the Gentiles in Christ Jesus, that we might receive the promise of the Spirit through faith.

[2] **Deut. 21:22–23.** If a man has committed a sin deserving of death, and he is put to death, and you hang him on a tree, his body shall not remain over-

night on the tree, but you shall surely bury him that day, so that you do not defile the land which the LORD your God is giving you as an inheritance; for he who is hanged is accursed of God.

✛ **Phil. 2:8.** And being found in appearance as a man, He humbled Himself and became obedient to the point of death, even the death of the cross.

LORD'S DAY 16

40. Why was it necessary for Christ to suffer "death"?

Because the justice and truth[1] of God required that satisfaction for our sins could be made in no other way than by the death of the Son of God.[2]

[1] **Gen. 2:17.** But of the tree of the knowledge of good and evil you shall not eat, for in the day that you eat of it you shall surely die.

[2] **Heb. 2:9.** But we see Jesus, who was made a little lower than the angels, for the suffering of death crowned with glory and honor, that He, by the grace of God, might taste death for everyone.

✛ **Rom. 6:23.** For the wages of sin is death, but the gift of God is eternal life in Christ Jesus our Lord.

41. Why was He "buried"?

To show thereby that He was really dead.[1]

[1] **Matt. 27:59–60.** When Joseph had taken the body, he wrapped it in a clean linen cloth, and laid it in his new tomb which he had hewn out of the rock; and he rolled a large stone against the door of the tomb, and departed.

Jn. 19:38–42. After this, Joseph of Arimathea, being a disciple of Jesus, but secretly, for fear of the Jews, asked Pilate that he might take away the body of Jesus; and Pilate gave him permission. So he came and took the body of Jesus. And Nicodemus, who at first came to Jesus by night, also came, bringing a mixture of myrrh and aloes, about a hundred pounds. Then they took the body of Jesus, and bound it in strips of linen with the spices, as the custom of the Jews is to bury. Now in the place where He was crucified there was a garden, and in the garden a new tomb in which no one had yet been laid. So there they laid Jesus, because of the Jews' Preparation Day, for the tomb was nearby.

Acts 13:29. Now when they had fulfilled all that was written concerning Him, they took Him down from the tree and laid Him in a tomb.

42. Since, then, Christ died for us, why must we also die?

Our death is not a satisfaction for our sin, but only a dying to sin and an entering into eternal life.[1]

[1] Jn. 5:24. Most assuredly, I say to you, he who hears My word and believes in Him who sent Me has everlasting life, and shall not come into judgment, but has passed from death into life.

Phil. 1:23. For I am hard-pressed between the two, having a desire to depart and be with Christ, which is far better.

Rom. 7:24–25. O wretched man that I am! Who will deliver me from this body of death? I thank God—through Jesus Christ our Lord! So then, with the mind I myself serve the law of God, but with the flesh the law of sin.

43. What further benefit do we receive from the sacrifice and death of Christ on the cross?

That by His power our old man is with Him crucified, slain, and buried;[1] so that the evil lusts of the flesh may no more reign in us,[2] but that we may offer ourselves unto Him a sacrifice of thanksgiving.[3]

[1] Rom. 6:6–8. Knowing this, that our old man was crucified with Him, that the body of sin might be done away with, that we should no longer be slaves of sin. For he who has died has been freed from sin. Now if we died with Christ, we believe that we shall also live with Him.

Col. 2:12. Buried with Him in baptism, in which you also were raised with Him through faith in the working of God, who raised Him from the dead.

[2] Rom. 6:12. Therefore do not let sin reign in your mortal body, that you should obey it in its lusts.

[3] Rom. 12:1. I beseech you therefore, brethren, by the mercies of God, that you present your bodies a living sacrifice, holy, acceptable to God, which is your reasonable service.

✢ 2 Cor. 5:15. And He died for all, that those who live should live no longer for themselves, but for Him who died for them and rose again.

44. Why is it added: "He descended into hell"?

That in my greatest temptations I may be assured that Christ my Lord, by His inexpressible anguish, pains, and terrors, which He suffered in His soul on the cross and before, has redeemed me from the anguish and torment of hell.[1]

[1] **Isa. 53:10.** Yet it pleased the LORD to bruise Him; He has put Him to grief. When You make His soul an offering for sin, He shall see His seed, He shall prolong His days, and the pleasure of the LORD shall prosper in His hand.

   Matt. 27:46. And about the ninth hour Jesus cried out with a loud voice, saying, "Eli, Eli, lama sabachthani?" that is, "My God, My God, why have You forsaken Me?"

✢ **Ps. 18:5.** The sorrows of Sheol surrounded me; the snares of death confronted me.

✢ **Ps. 116:3.** The pains of death surrounded me, and the pangs of Sheol laid hold of me; I found trouble and sorrow.

LORD'S DAY 17

45. What benefit do we receive from the "resurrection" of Christ?

First, by His resurrection He has overcome death, that He might make us partakers of the righteousness which He has obtained for us by His death.[2] *Second,* by His power we are also now raised up to a new life.[2] *Third,* the resurrection of Christ is to us a sure pledge of our blessed resurrection.[3]

[1] **1 Cor. 15:15, 17.** Yes, and we are found false witnesses of God, because we have testified of God that He raised up Christ, whom He did not raise up—if in fact the dead do not rise. ... And if Christ is not risen, your faith is futile; you are still in your sins!

   1 Cor. 54–55. So when this corruptible has put on incorruption, and this mortal has put on immortality, then shall be brought to pass the saying that is written: "Death is swallowed up in victory. O Death, where is your sting? O Hades, where is your victory?"

   Rom. 4:25. Who was delivered up because of our offenses, and was raised because of our justification.

1 Pet. 1:3–4, 21. Blessed be the God and Father of our Lord Jesus Christ, who according to His abundant mercy has begotten us again to a living hope through the resurrection of Jesus Christ from the dead, to an inheritance incorruptible and undefiled and that does not fade away, reserved in heaven for you, ... who through Him believe in God, who raised Him from the dead and gave Him glory, so that your faith and hope are in God.

[2] **Rom. 6:4.** Therefore we were buried with Him through baptism into death, that just as Christ was raised from the dead by the glory of the Father, even so we also should walk in newness of life.

Col. 3:1–4. If then you were raised with Christ, seek those things which are above, where Christ is, sitting at the right hand of God. Set your mind on things above, not on things on the earth. For you died, and your life is hidden with Christ in God. When Christ who is our life appears, then you also will appear with Him in glory.

Eph. 2:5. Even when we were dead in trespasses, made us alive together with Christ (by grace you have been saved).

[3] **1 Cor. 15:12.** Now if Christ is preached that He has been raised from the dead, how do some among you say that there is no resurrection of the dead?

Rom. 8:11. But if the Spirit of Him who raised Jesus from the dead dwells in you, He who raised Christ from the dead will also give life to your mortal bodies through His Spirit who dwells in you.

✣ **1 Cor. 15:20–21.** But now Christ is risen from the dead, and has become the firstfruits of those who have fallen asleep. For since by man came death, by Man also came the resurrection of the dead.

46. What do you understand by the words "He ascended into heaven"?

That Christ, in the sight of His disciples, was taken up from the earth into heaven,[1] and continues there in our behalf [2] until He shall come again to judge the living and the dead.[3]

[1] **Acts 1:9.** Now when He had spoken these things, while they watched, He was taken up, and a cloud received Him out of their sight.

Matt. 26:64. Jesus said to him, "It is as you said. Nevertheless, I say to you, hereafter you will see the Son of Man sitting at the right hand of the Power, and coming on the clouds of heaven."

Mk. 16:19. So then, after the Lord had spoken to them, He was received up into heaven, and sat down at the right hand of God.

Lk. 24:51. Now it came to pass, while He blessed them, that He was parted from them and carried up into heaven.

[2] Heb. 4:14. Seeing then that we have a great High Priest who has passed through the heavens, Jesus the Son of God, let us hold fast our confession.

Heb. 7:24–25. But He, because He continues forever, has an unchangeable priesthood. Therefore He is also able to save to the uttermost those who come to God through Him, since He always lives to make intercession for them.

Heb. 9:11. But Christ came as High Priest of the good things to come, with the greater and more perfect tabernacle not made with hands, that is, not of this creation.

Rom. 8:34. Who is he who condemns? It is Christ who died, and furthermore is also risen, who is even at the right hand of God, who also makes intercession for us.

Eph. 4:10. He who descended is also the One who ascended far above all the heavens, that He might fill all things.

[3] Acts 1:11. Who also said, "Men of Galilee, why do you stand gazing up into heaven? This same Jesus, who was taken up from you into heaven, will so come in like manner as you saw Him go into heaven."

Matt. 24:30. Then the sign of the Son of Man will appear in heaven, and then all the tribes of the earth will mourn, and they will see the Son of Man coming on the clouds of heaven with power and great glory.

✠ Acts 3:20–21. And that He may send Jesus Christ, who was preached to you before, whom heaven must receive until the times of restoration of all things, which God has spoken by the mouth of all His holy prophets since the world began.

47. But is not Christ with us even unto the end of the world, as He has promised?[1]

Christ is true man and true God. According to His human nature He is now not on earth,[2] but according to His Godhead, majesty, grace, and Spirit, He is at no time absent from us.[3]

[1] Matt. 28:20. Teaching them to observe all things that I have commanded you; and lo, I am with you always, even to the end of the age. Amen.

[2] Matt. 26:11. For you have the poor with you always, but Me you do not have always.

Jn. 16:28. I came forth from the Father and have come into the world. Again, I leave the world and go to the Father.

Jn. 17:11. Now I am no longer in the world, but these are in the world, and I come to You. Holy Father, keep through Your name those whom You have given Me, that they may be one as We are.

[3] **Jn. 14:17–18.** The Spirit of truth, whom the world cannot receive, because it neither sees Him nor knows Him; but you know Him, for He dwells with you and will be in you. I will not leave you orphans; I will come to you.

Jn. 16:13. However, when He, the Spirit of truth, has come, He will guide you into all truth; for He will not speak on His own authority, but whatever He hears He will speak; and He will tell you things to come.

Eph. 4:8. Therefore He says: "When He ascended on high, He led captivity captive, and gave gifts to men."

✢ **Matt. 18:20.** For where two or three are gathered together in My name, I am there in the midst of them.

✢ **Heb. 8:4.** For if He were on earth, He would not be a priest, since there are priests who offer the gifts according to the law.

48. But are not, in this way, the two natures in Christ separated from one another, if the manhood is not wherever the Godhead is?

Not at all, for since the Godhead is incomprehensible and everywhere present,[1] it must follow that the same is not limited with the human nature He assumed, and yet remains personally united to it.[2]

[1] **Acts 7:49.** Heaven is My throne, and earth is My footstool. What house will you build for Me? says the Lord, or what is the place of My rest?

Jer. 23:24. "Can anyone hide himself in secret places, so I shall not see him?" says the Lord; "Do I not fill heaven and earth?" says the Lord.

[2] **Col. 2:9.** For in Him dwells all the fullness of the Godhead bodily.

Jn. 3:13. No one has ascended to heaven but He who came down from heaven, that is, the Son of Man who is in heaven.

Jn. 11:15. And I am glad for your sakes that I was not there, that you may believe. Nevertheless let us go to him.

Matt. 28:6. He is not here; for He is risen, as He said. Come, see the place where the Lord lay.

✢ **Jn. 1:48.** Nathanael said to Him, "How do You know me?" Jesus answered and said to him, "Before Philip called you, when you were under the fig tree, I saw you."

LORD'S DAY 18

49. What benefit do we receive from Christ's ascension into heaven?

First, that He is our Advocate in the presence of His Father in heaven.[1] *Second,* that we have our flesh in heaven as a sure pledge, that He as the Head, will also take us, His members, up to Himself.[2] *Third,* that He sends us His Spirit as an earnest,[3] by whose power we seek those things which are above, where Christ sits at the right hand of God, and not things on the earth.[4]

[1] **1 Jn. 2:1.** My little children, these things I write to you, so that you may not sin. And if anyone sins, we have an Advocate with the Father, Jesus Christ the righteous.

Rom. 8:34. Who is he who condemns? It is Christ who died, and furthermore is also risen, who is even at the right hand of God, who also makes intercession for us.

[2] **Jn. 14:2.** In My Father's house are many mansions; if it were not so, I would have told you. I go to prepare a place for you.

Jn. 20:17. Jesus said to her, "Do not cling to Me, for I have not yet ascended to My Father; but go to My brethren and say to them, 'I am ascending to My Father and your Father, and to My God and your God.'"

Eph. 2:6. And raised us up together, and made us sit together in the heavenly places in Christ Jesus.

[3] **Jn. 14:16.** And I will pray the Father, and He will give you another Helper, that He may abide with you forever.

Acts 2:33. Therefore being exalted to the right hand of God, and having received from the Father the promise of the Holy Spirit, He poured out this which you now see and hear.

2 Cor. 5:5. Now He who has prepared us for this very thing is God, who also has given us the Spirit as a guarantee.

[4] **Col. 3:1.** If then you were raised with Christ, seek those things which are above, where Christ is, sitting at the right hand of God.

✤ **Jn. 14:3.** And if I go and prepare a place for you, I will come again and receive you to Myself; that where I am, there you may be also.

✤ **Heb. 9:24.** For Christ has not entered the holy places made with hands, which are copies of the true, but into heaven itself, now to appear in the presence of God for us.

50. Why is it added: "And sits at the right hand of God"?

Because Christ ascended into heaven for this end, that He might there appear as the Head of His Church,[1] by whom the Father governs all things.[2]

[1] **Eph. 1:20–23.** Which He worked in Christ when He raised Him from the dead and seated Him at His right hand in the heavenly places, far above all principality and power and might and dominion, and every name that is named, not only in this age but also in that which is to come. And He put all things under His feet, and gave Him to be head over all things to the church, which is His body, the fullness of Him who fills all in all.

Col. 1:18. And He is the head of the body, the church, who is the beginning, the firstborn from the dead, that in all things He may have the preeminence.

[2] **Jn. 5:22.** For the Father judges no one, but has committed all judgment to the Son.

✤ **1 Pet. 3:22.** Who has gone into heaven and is at the right hand of God, angels and authorities and powers having been made subject to Him.

✤ **Ps. 110:1.** The LORD said to my Lord, "Sit at My right hand, till I make Your enemies Your footstool."

LORD'S DAY 19

51. What does this glory of Christ, our Head, profit us?

First, that by His Holy Spirit He pours out heavenly gifts upon us, His members;[1] *then*, that by His power He defends and preserves us against all enemies.[2]

[1] **Eph. 4:10–12.** He who descended is also the One who ascended far above all the heavens, that He might fill all things.) And He Himself gave some to be apostles, some prophets, some evangelists, and some pastors and teach-

ers, for the equipping of the saints for the work of ministry, for the edifying of the body of Christ.

[2] **Ps. 2:9.** You shall break them with a rod of iron; You shall dash them to pieces like a potter's vessel.

Jn. 10:28–30. And I give them eternal life, and they shall never perish; neither shall anyone snatch them out of My hand. My Father, who has given them to Me, is greater than all; and no one is able to snatch them out of My Father's hand. I and My Father are one.

✢ **1 Cor. 15:25–26.** For He must reign till He has put all enemies under His feet. The last enemy that will be destroyed is death.

✢ **Acts 2:33.** Therefore being exalted to the right hand of God, and having received from the Father the promise of the Holy Spirit, He poured out this which you now see and hear.

52. What comfort is it to you that Christ "shall come to judge the living and the dead"?

That in all my sorrows and persecutions, I, with uplifted head, look for the very One who offered Himself for me to the judgment of God, and removed all curse from me, to come as Judge from heaven,[1] who shall cast all His and my enemies into everlasting condemnation,[2] but shall take me with all His chosen ones to Himself into heavenly joy and glory.[3]

[1] **Lk. 21:28.** Now when these things begin to happen, look up and lift up your heads, because your redemption draws near.

Rom. 8:23–24. Not only that, but we also who have the firstfruits of the Spirit, even we ourselves groan within ourselves, eagerly waiting for the adoption, the redemption of our body. For we were saved in this hope, but hope that is seen is not hope; for why does one still hope for what he sees?

Phil. 3:20–21. For our citizenship is in heaven, from which we also eagerly wait for the Savior, the Lord Jesus Christ, who will transform our lowly body that it may be conformed to His glorious body, according to the working by which He is able even to subdue all things to Himself.

Tit. 2:13. Looking for the blessed hope and glorious appearing of our great God and Savior Jesus Christ.

[2] **2 Thess. 1:6, 10.** Since it is a righteous thing with God to repay with tribulation those who trouble you, ... when He comes, in that Day, to be glorified in His saints and to be admired among all those who believe, because our testimony among you was believed.

1 Thess. 4:16–18. For the Lord Himself will descend from heaven with a shout, with the voice of an archangel, and with the trumpet of God. And the dead in Christ will rise first. Then we who are alive and remain shall be caught up together with them in the clouds to meet the Lord in the air. And thus we shall always be with the Lord. Therefore comfort one another with these words.

Matt. 25:41. Then He will also say to those on the left hand, "Depart from Me, you cursed, into the everlasting fire prepared for the devil and his angels."

[3] **Acts 1:10–11.** And while they looked steadfastly toward heaven as He went up, behold, two men stood by them in white apparel, who also said, "Men of Galilee, why do you stand gazing up into heaven? This same Jesus, who was taken up from you into heaven, will so come in like manner as you saw Him go into heaven."

✢ **Heb. 9:28.** So Christ was offered once to bear the sins of many. To those who eagerly wait for Him He will appear a second time, apart from sin, for salvation.

God the Holy Spirit

LORD'S DAY 20

53. What do you believe concerning the "Holy Spirit"?

First, that He is co-eternal God with the Father and the Son.[1] *Second,* that He is also given unto me:[2] by true faith makes me a partaker of Christ and all His benefits,[3] comforts me,[4] and shall abide with me forever.[5]

[1] **Gen. 1:2.** The earth was without form, and void; and darkness was on the face of the deep. And the Spirit of God was hovering over the face of the waters.

Isa. 48:16. Come near to Me, hear this: I have not spoken in secret from the beginning; from the time that it was, I was there. And now the Lord GOD and His Spirit have sent Me.

1 Cor. 3:16. Do you not know that you are the temple of God and that the Spirit of God dwells in you?

1 Cor. 6:19. Or do you not know that your body is the temple of the Holy Spirit who is in you, whom you have from God, and you are not your own?

Acts 5:3–4. But Peter said, "Ananias, why has Satan filled your heart to lie to the Holy Spirit and keep back part of the price of the land for yourself? While it remained, was it not your own? And after it was sold, was it not in your own control? Why have you conceived this thing in your heart? You have not lied to men but to God."

[2] **Matt. 28:19.** Go therefore and make disciples of all the nations, baptizing them in the name of the Father and of the Son and of the Holy Spirit.

2 Cor. 1:21–22. Now He who establishes us with you in Christ and has anointed us is God, who also has sealed us and given us the Spirit in our hearts as a guarantee.

[3] **1 Pet. 1:2.** Elect according to the foreknowledge of God the Father, in sanctification of the Spirit, for obedience and sprinkling of the blood of Jesus Christ: grace to you and peace be multiplied.

1 Cor. 6:17. But he who is joined to the Lord is one spirit with Him.

[4] **Acts 9:31.** Then the churches throughout all Judea, Galilee, and Samaria had peace and were edified. And walking in the fear of the Lord and in the comfort of the Holy Spirit, they were multiplied.

[5] **Jn. 14:16.** And I will pray the Father, and He will give you another Helper, that He may abide with you forever.

1 Pet. 4:14. If you are reproached for the name of Christ, blessed are you, for the Spirit of glory and of God rests upon you. On their part He is blasphemed, but on your part He is glorified.

✢ **1 Jn. 4:13.** By this we know that we abide in Him, and He in us, because He has given us of His Spirit.

✢ **Rom. 15:13.** Now may the God of hope fill you with all joy and peace in believing, that you may abound in hope by the power of the Holy Spirit.

LORD'S DAY 21

54. What do you believe concerning the "holy, catholic Church"?

That out of the whole human race,[1] from the beginning to the end of the world,[2] the Son of God,[3] by His Spirit and Word,[4] gathers, defends, and preserves for Himself unto everlasting life a chosen communion[5] in the unity of the true faith;[6] and that I am and forever shall remain a living member of this communion.[7]

[1] **Gen. 26:4.** And I will make your descendants multiply as the stars of heaven; I will give to your descendants all these lands; and in your seed all the nations of the earth shall be blessed.

[2] **Jn. 10:10.** The thief does not come except to steal, and to kill, and to destroy. I have come that they may have life, and that they may have it more abundantly.

[3] **Eph. 1:10–13.** That in the dispensation of the fullness of the times He might gather together in one all things in Christ, both which are in heaven and which are on earth—in Him, in whom also we have obtained an inheritance, being predestined according to the purpose of Him who works all things according to the counsel of His will, that we who first trusted in Christ should be to the praise of His glory. In Him you also trusted, after you heard the word of truth, the gospel of your salvation; in whom also, having believed, you were sealed with the Holy Spirit of promise.

[4] **Rom. 1:16.** For I am not ashamed of the gospel of Christ, for it is the power of God to salvation for everyone who believes, for the Jew first and also for the Greek.

Isa. 59:21. "As for Me," says the LORD, "this is My covenant with them: My Spirit who is upon you, and My words which I have put in your mouth, shall not depart from your mouth, nor from the mouth of your descendants, nor from the mouth of your descendants' descendants," says the LORD, "from this time and forevermore."

Rom. 10:14–17. How then shall they call on Him in whom they have not believed? And how shall they believe in Him of whom they have not heard? And how shall they hear without a preacher? And how shall they preach unless they are sent? As it is written: "How beautiful are the feet of those who preach the gospel of peace, who bring glad tidings of good things!" But they have not all obeyed the gospel. For Isaiah says, "LORD, who has believed our report?" So then faith comes by hearing, and hearing by the word of God.

Eph. 5:26. That He might sanctify and cleanse her with the washing of water by the word.

[5] **Rom. 8:29–30.** For whom He foreknew, He also predestined to be conformed to the image of His Son, that He might be the firstborn among many brethren. Moreover whom He predestined, these He also called; whom He called, these He also justified; and whom He justified, these He also glorified.

Matt. 16:18. And I also say to you that you are Peter, and on this rock I will build My church, and the gates of Hades shall not prevail against it.

Eph. 4:3–6. Endeavoring to keep the unity of the Spirit in the bond of peace. There is one body and one Spirit, just as you were called in one hope of your calling; one Lord, one faith, one baptism; one God and Father of all, who is above all, and through all, and in you all.

[6] **Acts 2:46.** So continuing daily with one accord in the temple, and breaking bread from house to house, they ate their food with gladness and simplicity of heart.

Ps. 71:18. Now also when I am old and grayheaded, O God, do not forsake me, until I declare Your strength to this generation, Your power to everyone who is to come.

1 Cor. 11:26. For as often as you eat this bread and drink this cup, you proclaim the Lord's death till He comes.

Jn. 10:28–30. And I give them eternal life, and they shall never perish; neither shall anyone snatch them out of My hand. My Father, who has given them to Me, is greater than all; and no one is able to snatch them out of My Father's hand. I and My Father are one.

1 Cor. 1:8–9. Who will also confirm you to the end, that you may be blameless in the day of our Lord Jesus Christ. God is faithful, by whom you were called into the fellowship of His Son, Jesus Christ our Lord.

[7] **1 Jn. 3:21.** Beloved, if our heart does not condemn us, we have confidence toward God.

1 Jn. 2:19. They went out from us, but they were not of us; for if they had been of us, they would have continued with us; but they went out that they might be made manifest, that none of them were of us.

✢ **Gal. 3:28.** There is neither Jew nor Greek, there is neither slave nor free, there is neither male nor female; for you are all one in Christ Jesus.

55. What do you understand by the "communion of saints"?

First, that believers, one and all, as members of the Lord Jesus Christ, are partakers with Him in all His treasures and gifts;[1] *second,* that each one must feel himself bound to use his gifts readily and cheerfully for the advantage and welfare of other members.[2]

[1] **1 Jn. 1:3.** That which we have seen and heard we declare to you, that you also may have fellowship with us; and truly our fellowship is with the Father and with His Son Jesus Christ.

[2] **1 Cor. 12:12–13, 21.** For as the body is one and has many members, but all the members of that one body, being many, are one body, so also is Christ. For by one Spirit we were all baptized into one body—whether Jews or

Greeks, whether slaves or free—and have all been made to drink into one Spirit.

1 Cor. 12:21. And the eye cannot say to the hand, "I have no need of you"; nor again the head to the feet, "I have no need of you."

1 Cor. 13:5–6. (Love) does not behave rudely, does not seek its own, is not provoked, thinks no evil; does not rejoice in iniquity, but rejoices in the truth.

Phil. 2:4–6. Let each of you look out not only for his own interests, but also for the interests of others. Let this mind be in you which was also in Christ Jesus, who, being in the form of God, did not consider it robbery to be equal with God.

✢ **Heb. 3:14.** For we have become partakers of Christ if we hold the beginning of our confidence steadfast to the end.

56. What do you believe concerning the "forgiveness of sins"?

That God, for the sake of Christ's satisfaction,[1] will no more remember my sins, nor the sinful nature with which I have to struggle all my life long;[2] but graciously imputes to me the righteousness of Christ, that I may nevermore come into condemnation.[3]

[1] **1 Jn. 2:2.** And He Himself is the propitiation for our sins, and not for ours only but also for the whole world.

[2] **2 Cor. 5:19, 21.** That is, that God was in Christ reconciling the world to Himself, not imputing their trespasses to them, and has committed to us the word of reconciliation. ... For He made Him who knew no sin to be sin for us, that we might become the righteousness of God in Him.

Rom. 7:24–25. O wretched man that I am! Who will deliver me from this body of death? I thank God—through Jesus Christ our Lord! So then, with the mind I myself serve the law of God, but with the flesh the law of sin.

Ps. 103:3, 10, 12. Who forgives all your iniquities, who heals all your diseases. ... He has not dealt with us according to our sins, nor punished us according to our iniquities. ... As far as the east is from the west, so far has He removed our transgressions from us.

Jer. 31:34. No more shall every man teach his neighbor, and every man his brother, saying, "Know the LORD," for they all shall know Me, from the least of them to the greatest of them, says the LORD. For I will forgive their iniquity, and their sin I will remember no more.

Rom. 8:1–4. There is therefore now no condemnation to those who are in Christ Jesus, who do not walk according to the flesh, but according to the Spirit. For the law of the Spirit of life in Christ Jesus has made me free from the law of sin and death. For what the law could not do in that it was weak through the flesh, God did by sending His own Son in the likeness of sinful flesh, on account of sin: He condemned sin in the flesh, that the righteous requirement of the law might be fulfilled in us who do not walk according to the flesh but according to the Spirit.

[3] Jn. 3:18. He who believes in Him is not condemned; but he who does not believe is condemned already, because he has not believed in the name of the only begotten Son of God.

✢ Eph. 1:7. In Him we have redemption through His blood, the forgiveness of sins, according to the riches of His grace.

✢ Rom. 4:7–8. Blessed are those whose lawless deeds are forgiven, and whose sins are covered; blessed is the man to whom the Lord shall not impute sin.

✢ Rom. 7:18. For I know that in me (that is, in my flesh) nothing good dwells; for to will is present with me, but how to perform what is good I do not find.

Lord's Day 22

57. What comfort do you receive from the "resurrection of the body"?

That not only my soul after this life shall be immediately taken up to Christ its Head,[1] but also that this my body, raised by the power of Christ, shall be reunited with my soul, and made like the glorious body of Christ.[2]

[1] Lk. 23:43. And Jesus said to him, "Assuredly, I say to you, today you will be with Me in Paradise."

Phil. 1:21–23. For to me, to live is Christ, and to die is gain. But if I live on in the flesh, this will mean fruit from my labor; yet what I shall choose I cannot tell. For I am hard-pressed between the two, having a desire to depart and be with Christ, which is far better.

[2] 1 Cor. 15:53–54. For this corruptible must put on incorruption, and this mortal must put on immortality. So when this corruptible has put on incorruption, and this mortal has put on immortality, then shall be brought to pass the saying that is written: "Death is swallowed up in victory."

Job 19:25–27. For I know that my Redeemer lives, and He shall stand at last on the earth; and after my skin is destroyed, this I know, that in my flesh I shall see God, whom I shall see for myself, and my eyes shall behold, and not another. How my heart yearns within me!

1 Jn. 3:2. Beloved, now we are children of God; and it has not yet been revealed what we shall be, but we know that when He is revealed, we shall be like Him, for we shall see Him as He is.

58. What comfort do you receive from the article "life everlasting"?

That, inasmuch as I now feel in my heart the beginning of eternal joy,[1] I shall after this life possess complete blessedness, such as eye has not seen, nor ear heard, neither has entered into the heart of man,[2] therein to praise God forever.[3]

[1] 2 Cor. 5:2–3. For in this we groan, earnestly desiring to be clothed with our habitation which is from heaven, if indeed, having been clothed, we shall not be found naked.

[2] 1 Cor. 2:9. But as it is written: "Eye has not seen, nor ear heard, Nor have entered into the heart of man the things which God has prepared for those who love Him."

[3] Jn. 17:3. And this is eternal life, that they may know You, the only true God, and Jesus Christ whom You have sent.

✣ Rom. 8:23. Not only that, but we also who have the firstfruits of the Spirit, even we ourselves groan within ourselves, eagerly waiting for the adoption, the redemption of our body.

✣ 1 Pet. 1:8. Whom having not seen you love. Though now you do not see Him, yet believing, you rejoice with joy inexpressible and full of glory.

Lord's Day 23

59. What does it help you now, that you believe all this?

That I am righteous in Christ before God, and an heir of eternal life.[1]

[1] Hab. 2:4. Behold the proud, His soul is not upright in him; but the just shall live by his faith.

Rom. 1:17. For in it the righteousness of God is revealed from faith to faith; as it is written, "The just shall live by faith."

Jn. 3:36. He who believes in the Son has everlasting life; and he who does not believe the Son shall not see life, but the wrath of God abides on him.

✛ **Tit. 3:7.** That having been justified by His grace we should become heirs according to the hope of eternal life.

✛ **Rom. 5:1.** Therefore, having been justified by faith, we have peace with God through our Lord Jesus Christ.

✛ **Rom. 8:16.** The Spirit Himself bears witness with our spirit that we are children of God.

60. How are you righteous before God?

Only by true faith in Jesus Christ:[1] that is, although my conscience accuses me, that I have grievously sinned against all the commandments of God, and have never kept any of them,[2] and am still prone always to all evil;[3] yet God, without any merit of mine,[4] of mere grace,[5] grants and imputes to me the perfect satisfaction,[6] righteousness, and holiness of Christ,[7] as if I had never committed nor had any sins, and had myself accomplished all the obedience which Christ has fulfilled for me;[8] if only I accept such benefit with a believing heart.[9]

[1] **Rom. 3:21–25.** But now the righteousness of God apart from the law is revealed, being witnessed by the Law and the Prophets, even the righteousness of God, through faith in Jesus Christ, to all and on all who believe. For there is no difference; for all have sinned and fall short of the glory of God, being justified freely by His grace through the redemption that is in Christ Jesus, whom God set forth as a propitiation by His blood, through faith, to demonstrate His righteousness, because in His forbearance God had passed over the sins that were previously committed.

Gal. 2:16. Knowing that a man is not justified by the works of the law but by faith in Jesus Christ, even we have believed in Christ Jesus, that we might be justified by faith in Christ and not by the works of the law; for by the works of the law no flesh shall be justified.

Eph. 2:8–9. For by grace you have been saved through faith, and that not of yourselves; it is the gift of God, not of works, lest anyone should boast.

Phil. 3:9. And be found in Him, not having my own righteousness, which is from the law, but that which is through faith in Christ, the righteousness which is from God by faith.

[2] **Rom. 3:9–10.** What then? Are we better than they? Not at all. For we have previously charged both Jews and Greeks that they are all under sin. As it is written: "There is none righteous, no, not one."

[3] **Rom. 7:23.** But I see another law in my members, warring against the law of my mind, and bringing me into captivity to the law of sin which is in my members.

[4] **Tit. 3:5.** Not by works of righteousness which we have done, but according to His mercy He saved us, through the washing of regeneration and renewing of the Holy Spirit.

[5] **Rom. 3:24.** Being justified freely by His grace through the redemption that is in Christ Jesus.

Eph. 2:8. For by grace you have been saved through faith, and that not of yourselves; it is the gift of God.

[6] **1 Jn. 2:2.** And He Himself is the propitiation for our sins, and not for ours only but also for the whole world.

[7] **1 Jn. 2:1.** My little children, these things I write to you, so that you may not sin. And if anyone sins, we have an Advocate with the Father, Jesus Christ the righteous.

Rom. 4:4–5. Now to him who works, the wages are not counted as grace but as debt. But to him who does not work but believes on Him who justifies the ungodly, his faith is accounted for righteousness.

2 Cor. 5:19. That is, that God was in Christ reconciling the world to Himself, not imputing their trespasses to them, and has committed to us the word of reconciliation.

[8] **2 Cor. 5:21.** For He made Him who knew no sin to be sin for us, that we might become the righteousness of God in Him.

[9] **Jn. 3:18.** He who believes in Him is not condemned; but he who does not believe is condemned already, because he has not believed in the name of the only begotten Son of God.

✢ **Rom. 3:28.** Therefore we conclude that a man is justified by faith apart from the deeds of the law.

✢ **Rom. 10:10.** For with the heart one believes unto righteousness, and with the mouth confession is made unto salvation.

61. Why do you say that you are righteous by faith only?

Not that I am acceptable to God on account of the worthiness of my faith, but because only the satisfaction, righteousness, and holiness of Christ is my righteousness before God;[1] and I can receive the same and make it my own in no other way than by faith only.[2]

[1] **1 Cor. 1:30.** But of Him you are in Christ Jesus, who became for us wisdom from God—and righteousness and sanctification and redemption.

1 Cor. 2:2. For I determined not to know anything among you except Jesus Christ and Him crucified.

[2] **1 Jn. 5:10.** He who believes in the Son of God has the witness in himself; he who does not believe God has made Him a liar, because he has not believed the testimony that God has given of His Son.

✢ **Isa. 53:5.** But He was wounded for our transgressions, He was bruised for our iniquities; the chastisement for our peace was upon Him, and by His stripes we are healed.

✢ **Gal. 3:22.** But the Scripture has confined all under sin, that the promise by faith in Jesus Christ might be given to those who believe.

✢ **Rom. 4:16.** Therefore it is of faith that it might be according to grace, so that the promise might be sure to all the seed, not only to those who are of the law, but also to those who are of the faith of Abraham, who is the father of us all.

LORD'S DAY 24

62. But why cannot our good works be the whole or part of our righteousness before God?

Because the righteousness which can stand before the judgment seat of God must be perfect throughout and entirely conformable to the divine law,[1] but even our best works in this life are all imperfect and defiled with sin.[2]

[1] **Gal. 3:10.** For as many as are of the works of the law are under the curse; for it is written, "Cursed is everyone who does not continue in all things which are written in the book of the law, to do them."

Deut. 27:26. Cursed is the one who does not confirm all the words of this law. And all the people shall say, "Amen!"

[2] **Isa. 64:6.** But we are all like an unclean thing, and all our righteousnesses are like filthy rags. We all fade as a leaf, and our iniquities, like the wind, have taken us away.

✛ **Jas. 2:10.** For whoever shall keep the whole law, and yet stumble in one point, he is guilty of all.

✛ **Phil. 3:12.** Not that I have already attained, or am already perfected; but I press on, that I may lay hold of that for which Christ Jesus has also laid hold of me.

63. Do our good works merit nothing, even though it is God's will to reward them in this life and in that which is to come?

The reward comes not of merit, but of grace.[1]

[1] **Lk. 17:10.** So likewise you, when you have done all those things which you are commanded, say, "We are unprofitable servants. We have done what was our duty to do."

✛ **Rom. 11:6.** And if by grace, then it is no longer of works; otherwise grace is no longer grace. But if it is of works, it is no longer grace; otherwise work is no longer work.

64. But does not this doctrine make men careless and profane?

No, for it is impossible that those who are implanted into Christ by true faith, should not bring forth fruits of thankfulness.[1]

[1] **Matt. 7:18.** A good tree cannot bear bad fruit, nor can a bad tree bear good fruit.

✛ **Rom. 6:1–2.** What shall we say then? Shall we continue in sin that grace may abound? Certainly not! How shall we who died to sin live any longer in it?

✛ **Jn. 15:5.** I am the vine, you are the branches. He who abides in Me, and I in him, bears much fruit; for without Me you can do nothing.

The Sacraments

Lord's Day 25

65. Since, then, we are made partakers of Christ and all His benefits by faith only, where does this faith come from?

The Holy Spirit works faith in our hearts[1] by the preaching of the Holy Gospel, and confirms it by the use of the holy sacraments.[2]

[1] **Jn. 3:5.** Jesus answered, "Most assuredly, I say to you, unless one is born of water and the Spirit, he cannot enter the kingdom of God."

✢ **Rom. 10:17.** So then faith comes by hearing, and hearing by the word of God.

[2] **Rom. 4:11.** And he received the sign of circumcision, a seal of the righteousness of the faith which he had while still uncircumcised, that he might be the father of all those who believe, though they are uncircumcised, that righteousness might be imputed to them also.

✢ **Acts 8:37.** Then Philip said, "If you believe with all your heart, you may." And he answered and said, "I believe that Jesus Christ is the Son of God."

66. What are the sacraments?

The sacraments are visible holy signs and seals appointed by God for this end, that by their use He may the more fully declare and seal to us the promise of the Gospel, namely, that of free grace He grants us the forgiveness of sins and everlasting life for the sake of the one sacrifice of Christ accomplished on the cross.[1]

[1] **Gen. 17:11.** And you shall be circumcised in the flesh of your foreskins, and it shall be a sign of the covenant between Me and you.

Rom. 4:11. And he received the sign of circumcision, a seal of the righteousness of the faith which he had while still uncircumcised, that he might be the father of all those who believe, though they are uncircumcised, that righteousness might be imputed to them also.

Deut. 30:6. And the LORD your God will circumcise your heart and the heart of your descendants, to love the LORD your God with all your heart and with all your soul, that you may live.

Heb. 9:8–9. The Holy Spirit indicating this, that the way into the Holiest of All was not yet made manifest while the first tabernacle was still standing. It was symbolic for the present time in which both gifts and sacrifices are offered which cannot make him who performed the service perfect in regard to the conscience.

Ezek. 20:12. Moreover I also gave them My Sabbaths, to be a sign between them and Me, that they might know that I am the LORD who sanctifies them.

67. Are both the Word and the sacraments designed to direct our faith to the sacrifice of Christ on the cross as the only ground of our salvation?

Yes, truly, for the Holy Spirit teaches in the Gospel and assures us by the holy sacraments, that our whole salvation stands in the one sacrifice of Christ made for us on the cross.[1]

[1] **Rom. 6:3.** Or do you not know that as many of us as were baptized into Christ Jesus were baptized into His death?

✤ **Gal. 3:27.** For as many of you as were baptized into Christ have put on Christ.

✤ **Heb. 9:12.** Not with the blood of goats and calves, but with His own blood He entered the Most Holy Place once for all, having obtained eternal redemption.

✤ **Acts 2:41–42.** Then those who gladly received his word were baptized; and that day about three thousand souls were added to them. And they continued steadfastly in the apostles' doctrine and fellowship, in the breaking of bread, and in prayers.

68. How many sacraments has Christ instituted in the New Testament?

Two: Holy Baptism and the Holy Supper.

Holy Baptism

LORD'S DAY 26

69. How is it signified and sealed to you in Holy Baptism that you have part in the one sacrifice of Christ on the cross?

Thus: that Christ instituted this outward washing with water[1] and joined to it this promise,[2] that I am washed with His blood and Spirit from the pollution of my soul, that is, from all my sins, as certainly as I am washed outwardly with water, whereby commonly the filthiness of the body is taken away.[3]

[1] **Matt. 28:19–20.** Go therefore and make disciples of all the nations, baptizing them in the name of the Father and of the Son and of the Holy Spirit, teaching them to observe all things that I have commanded you; and lo, I am with you always, even to the end of the age. Amen.

Acts 2:38. Then Peter said to them, "Repent, and let every one of you be baptized in the name of Jesus Christ for the remission of sins; and you shall receive the gift of the Holy Spirit."

[2] **Matt. 3:11.** I indeed baptize you with water unto repentance, but He who is coming after me is mightier than I, whose sandals I am not worthy to carry. He will baptize you with the Holy Spirit and fire.

Mk. 16:16. He who believes and is baptized will be saved; but he who does not believe will be condemned.

Rom. 6:3–4. Or do you not know that as many of us as were baptized into Christ Jesus were baptized into His death? Therefore we were buried with Him through baptism into death, that just as Christ was raised from the dead by the glory of the Father, even so we also should walk in newness of life.

[3] **Mk. 1:4.** John came baptizing in the wilderness and preaching a baptism of repentance for the remission of sins.

70. What is it to be washed with the blood and Spirit of Christ?

It is to have the forgiveness of sins from God through grace, for the sake of Christ's blood, which He shed for us in His sacrifice on the cross;[1] and also to be renewed by the Holy Spirit and sanctified to be members of Christ, so that we may more and more die unto sin and lead holy and blameless lives.[2]

[1] **Heb. 12:24.** To Jesus the Mediator of the new covenant, and to the blood of sprinkling that speaks better things than that of Abel.

1 Pet. 1:2. Elect according to the foreknowledge of God the Father, in sanctification of the Spirit, for obedience and sprinkling of the blood of Jesus Christ: Grace to you and peace be multiplied.

Rev. 1:5. And from Jesus Christ, the faithful witness, the firstborn from the dead, and the ruler over the kings of the earth. To Him who loved us and washed us from our sins in His own blood.

Zech. 13:1. In that day a fountain shall be opened for the house of David and for the inhabitants of Jerusalem, for sin and for uncleanness.

Ezek. 36:25–27. Then I will sprinkle clean water on you, and you shall be clean; I will cleanse you from all your filthiness and from all your idols. I will give you a new heart and put a new spirit within you; I will take the heart of stone out of your flesh and give you a heart of flesh. I will put My Spirit within you and cause you to walk in My statutes, and you will keep My judgments and do them.

[2] **Jn. 1:33.** I did not know Him, but He who sent me to baptize with water said to me, "Upon whom you see the Spirit descending, and remaining on Him, this is He who baptizes with the Holy Spirit."

Jn. 3:3. Jesus answered and said to him, "Most assuredly, I say to you, unless one is born again, he cannot see the kingdom of God."

1 Cor. 6:11. And such were some of you. But you were washed, but you were sanctified, but you were justified in the name of the Lord Jesus and by the Spirit of our God.

1 Cor. 12:13. For by one Spirit we were all baptized into one body—whether Jews or Greeks, whether slaves or free—and have all been made to drink into one Spirit.

✢ **Heb. 9:14.** How much more shall the blood of Christ, who through the eternal Spirit offered Himself without spot to God, cleanse your conscience from dead works to serve the living God?

71. Where has Christ promised that we are as certainly washed with His blood and Spirit as with the water of Baptism?

In the institution of Baptism, which says, "*Go therefore and make disciples of all the nations, baptizing them in the name of the Father and of the Son and of the Holy Spirit.*"[1] "*He who believes and is baptized will be saved but he who does not believe will be condemned.*"[2] This promise is also repeated where Scripture calls Baptism the washing of regeneration[3] and the washing away of sins.[4]

[1] **Matt. 28:19.** Go therefore and make disciples of all the nations, baptizing them in the name of the Father and of the Son and of the Holy Spirit.

[2] **Mk. 16:16.** He who believes and is baptized will be saved; but he who does not believe will be condemned.

[3] **Tit. 3:5.** Not by works of righteousness which we have done, but according to His mercy He saved us, through the washing of regeneration and renewing of the Holy Spirit.

[4] **Acts 22:16.** And now why are you waiting? Arise and be baptized, and wash away your sins, calling on the name of the Lord.

LORD'S DAY 27

72. Is, then, the outward washing with water itself the washing away of sins?

No,[1] for only the blood of Jesus Christ and the Holy Spirit cleanse us from all sin.[2]

[1] **1 Pet. 3:21.** There is also an antitype which now saves us—baptism (not the removal of the filth of the flesh, but the answer of a good conscience toward God), through the resurrection of Jesus Christ.

Eph. 5:26. That He might sanctify and cleanse her with the washing of water by the word.

[2] **1 Jn. 1:7.** But if we walk in the light as He is in the light, we have fellowship with one another, and the blood of Jesus Christ His Son cleanses us from all sin.

1 Cor. 6:11. And such were some of you. But you were washed, but you were sanctified, but you were justified in the name of the Lord Jesus and by the Spirit of our God.

73. Why then does the Holy Spirit call Baptism the washing of regeneration and the washing away of sins?

God speaks thus with great cause, namely, not only to teach us thereby that just as the filthiness of the body is taken away by water, so our sins are taken away by the blood and Spirit of Christ;[1] but much more, that by this divine pledge and token He may assure us that we are as really washed from our sins spiritually as our bodies are washed with water.[2]

[1] **Rev. 7:14.** And I said to him, "Sir, you know." So he said to me, "These are the ones who come out of the great tribulation, and washed their robes and made them white in the blood of the Lamb."

[2] **Mk. 16:16.** He who believes and is baptized will be saved; but he who does not believe will be condemned.

✢ **Acts 2:38.** Then Peter said to them, "Repent, and let every one of you be baptized in the name of Jesus Christ for the remission of sins; and you shall receive the gift of the Holy Spirit."

74. Are infants also to be baptized?

Yes, for since they, as well as their parents, belong to the covenant and people of God,[1] and through the blood of Christ[2] both redemption from sin and the Holy Spirit, who works faith, are promised to them no less than to their parents,[3] they are also by Baptism, as a sign of the covenant, to be ingrafted into the Christian Church, and distinguished from the children of unbelievers,[4] as was done in the Old Testament by circumcision,[5] in place of which in the New Testament Baptism is appointed.[6]

[1] **Gen. 17:7.** And I will establish My covenant between Me and you and your descendants after you in their generations, for an everlasting covenant, to be God to you and your descendants after you.

[2] **Matt. 19:14.** But Jesus said, "Let the little children come to Me, and do not forbid them; for of such is the kingdom of heaven."

[3] **Lk. 1:14–15.** And you will have joy and gladness, and many will rejoice at his birth. For he will be great in the sight of the Lord, and shall drink neither wine nor strong drink. He will also be filled with the Holy Spirit, even from his mother's womb.

Ps. 22:10. I was cast upon You from birth. From My mother's womb You have been My God.

Acts 2:39. For the promise is to you and to your children, and to all who are afar off, as many as the Lord our God will call.

[4] Acts 10:47. Can anyone forbid water, that these should not be baptized who have received the Holy Spirit just as we have?

[5] Gen. 17:14. And the uncircumcised male child, who is not circumcised in the flesh of his foreskin, that person shall be cut off from his people; he has broken My covenant.

[6] Col. 2:11–13. In Him you were also circumcised with the circumcision made without hands, by putting off the body of the sins of the flesh, by the circumcision of Christ, buried with Him in baptism, in which you also were raised with Him through faith in the working of God, who raised Him from the dead. And you, being dead in your trespasses and the uncircumcision of your flesh, He has made alive together with Him, having forgiven you all trespasses.

The Holy Supper

LORD'S DAY 28

75. How is it signified and sealed to you in the Holy Supper that you partake of the one sacrifice of Christ on the cross and all His benefits?

Thus: that Christ has commanded me and all believers to eat of this broken bread and to drink of this cup in remembrance of Him, and has joined therewith these promises:[1] first, that His body was offered and broken on the cross for me and His blood shed for me, as certainly as I see with my eyes the bread of the Lord broken for me and the cup communicated to me; and further, that with His crucified body and shed blood He Himself feeds and nourishes my soul to everlasting life, as certainly as I receive from the hand of the minister and taste with my mouth the bread and cup of the Lord, which are given me as certain tokens of the body and blood of Christ.

[1] **Matt. 26:26–28.** And as they were eating, Jesus took bread, blessed and broke it, and gave it to the disciples and said, "Take, eat; this is My body." Then He took the cup, and gave thanks, and gave it to them, saying, "Drink from it, all of you. For this is My blood of the new covenant, which is shed for many for the remission of sins."

Mk. 14:22–24. And as they were eating, Jesus took bread, blessed and broke it, and gave it to them and said, "Take, eat; this is My body." Then He took the cup, and when He had given thanks He gave it to them, and they all drank from it. And He said to them, "This is My blood of the new covenant, which is shed for many."

Lk. 22:19–20. And He took bread, gave thanks and broke it, and gave it to them, saying, "This is My body which is given for you; do this in remembrance of Me." Likewise He also took the cup after supper, saying, "This cup is the new covenant in My blood, which is shed for you."

1 Cor. 10:16–17. The cup of blessing which we bless, is it not the communion of the blood of Christ? The bread which we break, is it not the communion of the body of Christ? For we, though many, are one bread and one body; for we all partake of that one bread.

1 Cor. 11:23–25. For I received from the Lord that which I also delivered to you: that the Lord Jesus on the same night in which He was betrayed took bread; and when He had given thanks, He broke it and said, "Take, eat; this is My body which is broken for you; do this in remembrance of Me." In the same manner He also took the cup after supper, saying, "This cup is the new covenant in My blood. This do, as often as you drink it, in remembrance of Me."

1 Cor. 12:13. For by one Spirit we were all baptized into one body— whether Jews or Greeks, whether slaves or free—and have all been made to drink into one Spirit.

76. What does it mean to eat the crucified body and drink the shed blood of Christ?

It means not only to embrace with a believing heart all the sufferings and death of Christ, and thereby to obtain the forgiveness of sins and life eternal;[1] but moreover, also, to be so united more and more to His sacred body by the Holy Spirit,[2] who dwells both in Christ and in us, that, although He is in heaven[3] and we on earth, we are nevertheless flesh of His flesh and bone of His bone,[4] and live and are governed forever by one Spirit, as members of the same body are governed by one soul.[5]

[1] **Jn. 6:35, 40, 47–48.** And Jesus said to them, "I am the bread of life. He who comes to Me shall never hunger, and he who believes in Me shall never thirst. ... And this is the will of Him who sent Me, that everyone who sees the Son and believes in Him may have everlasting life; and I will raise him up at the last day. ... Most assuredly, I say to you, he who believes in Me has everlasting life. I am the bread of life."

Jn. 6:50–54. This is the bread which comes down from heaven, that one may eat of it and not die. I am the living bread which came down from heaven. If anyone eats of this bread, he will live forever; and the bread that I shall give is My flesh, which I shall give for the life of the world. The Jews therefore quarreled among themselves, saying, "How can this Man give us His flesh to eat?" Then Jesus said to them, "Most assuredly, I say to you, unless you eat the flesh of the Son of Man and drink His blood, you have no life in you. Whoever eats My flesh and drinks My blood has eternal life, and I will raise him up at the last day."

[2] **Jn. 6:55–56.** For My flesh is food indeed, and My blood is drink indeed. He who eats My flesh and drinks My blood abides in Me, and I in him.

[3] **Acts 3:21.** Whom heaven must receive until the times of restoration of all things, which God has spoken by the mouth of all His holy prophets since the world began.

1 Cor. 11:26. For as often as you eat this bread and drink this cup, you proclaim the Lord's death till He comes.

[4] **Eph. 3:16–19.** That He would grant you, according to the riches of His glory, to be strengthened with might through His Spirit in the inner man, that Christ may dwell in your hearts through faith; that you, being rooted and grounded in love, may be able to comprehend with all the saints what is the width and length and depth and height—to know the love of Christ which passes knowledge; that you may be filled with all the fullness of God.

Eph. 5:29–30, 32. For no one ever hated his own flesh, but nourishes and cherishes it, just as the Lord does the church. For we are members of His body, of His flesh and of His bones. This is a great mystery, but I speak concerning Christ and the church.

1 Cor. 6:15, 17, 19. Do you not know that your bodies are members of Christ? Shall I then take the members of Christ and make them members of a harlot? Certainly not! ... But he who is joined to the Lord is one spirit with Him. ... Or do you not know that your body is the temple of the Holy Spirit who is in you, whom you have from God, and you are not your own?

1 Jn. 4:13. By this we know that we abide in Him, and He in us, because He has given us of His Spirit.

[5] **Jn. 14:23.** Jesus answered and said to him, "If anyone loves Me, he will keep My word; and My Father will love him, and We will come to him and make Our home with him."

Jn. 6:56–58. He who eats My flesh and drinks My blood abides in Me, and I in him. As the living Father sent Me, and I live because of the Father, so he who feeds on Me will live because of Me. This is the bread which came down from heaven—not as your fathers ate the manna, and are dead. He who eats this bread will live forever.

Jn. 15:1–6. I am the true vine, and My Father is the vinedresser. Every branch in Me that does not bear fruit He takes away; and every branch that bears fruit He prunes, that it may bear more fruit. You are already clean because of the word which I have spoken to you. Abide in Me, and I in you. As the branch cannot bear fruit of itself, unless it abides in the vine, neither can you, unless you abide in Me. I am the vine, you are the branches. He who abides in Me, and I in him, bears much fruit; for without Me you can do nothing. If anyone does not abide in Me, he is cast out as a branch and is withered; and they gather them and throw them into the fire, and they are burned.

Eph. 4:15–16. But, speaking the truth in love, may grow up in all things into Him who is the head—Christ—from whom the whole body, joined and knit together by what every joint supplies, according to the effective working by which every part does its share, causes growth of the body for the edifying of itself in love.

Jn. 6:63. It is the Spirit who gives life; the flesh profits nothing. The words that I speak to you are spirit, and they are life.

77. Where has Christ promised that He will thus feed and nourish believers with His body and blood as certainly as they eat of this broken bread and drink of this cup?

In the institution of the Supper, which says: *"The Lord Jesus on the same night in which He was betrayed took bread; and when He had given thanks, He broke it and said, 'Take, eat; this is My body which is broken for you; do this in remembrance of Me.' In the same manner He also took the cup after supper, saying, 'This cup is the new covenant in My blood. This do, as often as you drink it, in remembrance of Me.' For as often as you eat this bread and drink this cup, you proclaim the Lord's death till He comes."* [1] And this promise is also repeated by the Apostle Paul, where he says, *"The cup of blessing which we bless, is it not the communion of the blood of Christ? The bread which we break, is it not the communion of the body of Christ? Because there is one bread, so we being many are one body, for we are all partakers of that one bread."*[2]

[1] **1 Cor. 11:23.** For I received from the Lord that which I also delivered to you: that the Lord Jesus on the same night in which He was betrayed took bread; and when He had given thanks, He broke it and said, "Take, eat; this is My body which is broken for you; do this in remembrance of Me." In the same manner He also took the cup after supper, saying, "This cup is the new covenant in My blood. This do, as often as you drink it, in remembrance of Me."

[2] **1 Cor. 10:16–17.** The cup of blessing which we bless, is it not the communion of the blood of Christ? The bread which we break, is it not the communion of the body of Christ? For we, though many, are one bread and one body; for we all partake of that one bread.

LORD'S DAY 29

78. Do, then, the bread and the wine become the real body and blood of Christ?

No, but as the water in Baptism is not changed into the blood of Christ, nor becomes the washing away of sins itself, being only the divine token and assurance thereof,[1] so also in the Lord's Supper the sacred bread[2] does not become the body of Christ itself, though agreeably to the nature and usage of sacraments it is called the body of Christ.[3]

[1] **Matt. 26:29.** But I say to you, I will not drink of this fruit of the vine from now on until that day when I drink it new with you in My Father's kingdom.

[2] **1 Cor. 11:26–28.** For as often as you eat this bread and drink this cup, you proclaim the Lord's death till He comes. Therefore whoever eats this bread or drinks this cup of the Lord in an unworthy manner will be guilty of the body and blood of the Lord. But let a man examine himself, and so let him eat of the bread and drink of the cup.

[3] **Ex. 12:26–27.** And it shall be, when your children say to you, "What do you mean by this service?" that you shall say "It is the Passover sacrifice of the LORD, who passed over the houses of the children of Israel in Egypt when He struck the Egyptians and delivered our households." So the people bowed their heads and worshiped.

Ex. 12:43, 48. And the LORD said to Moses and Aaron, "This is the ordinance of the Passover: no foreigner shall eat it. ... And when a stranger dwells with you and wants to keep the Passover to the LORD, let all his males be circumcised, and then let him come near and keep it; and he shall be as a native of the land. For no uncircumcised person shall eat it."

1 Cor. 10:1–4. Moreover, brethren, I do not want you to be unaware that all our fathers were under the cloud, all passed through the sea, all were baptized into Moses in the cloud and in the sea, all ate the same spiritual food, and all drank the same spiritual drink. For they drank of that spiritual Rock that followed them, and that Rock was Christ.

79. Why then does Christ call the bread His body, and the cup His blood, or the new testament in His blood; and the Apostle Paul, the communion of the body and the blood of Christ?

Christ speaks thus with great cause, namely, not only to teach us thereby, that like as the bread and wine sustain this temporal life, so also His crucified body and shed blood are the true meat and drink of our souls unto life eternal;[1] but much more, by this visible sign and pledge to assure us that we are as really partakers of His true body and blood by the working of the Holy Spirit, as we receive by the mouth of the body these holy tokens in remembrance of Him;[2] and that all His sufferings and obedience are as certainly our own, as if we ourselves had suffered and done all in our own person.

[1] Jn. 6:51–55. (See Question 76.) I am the living bread which came down from heaven. If anyone eats of this bread, he will live forever; and the bread that I shall give is My flesh, which I shall give for the life of the world. The Jews therefore quarreled among themselves, saying, "How can this Man give us His flesh to eat?" Then Jesus said to them, "Most assuredly, I say to you, unless you eat the flesh of the Son of Man and drink His blood, you have no life in you. Whoever eats My flesh and drinks My blood has eternal life, and I will raise him up at the last day. For My flesh is food indeed, and My blood is drink indeed."

[2] 1 Cor. 10:16–17. (See Question 78.) The cup of blessing which we bless, is it not the communion of the blood of Christ? The bread which we break, is it not the communion of the body of Christ? For we, being many, are one bread and one body; for we all partake of that one bread.

LORD'S DAY 30

80. What difference is there between the Lord's Supper and the Pope's Mass?

The Lord's Supper testifies to us that we have full forgiveness of all our sins by the one sacrifice of Jesus Christ, which He Himself once accomplished on the cross;[1] and that by the Holy Spirit we are engrafted into Christ,[2] who, with His true body is now in heaven at the right hand of the Father,[3] and is there to be worshiped.[4] But the Mass teaches that the living and the dead do not have forgiveness of sins through the sufferings of Christ, unless Christ is still daily offered for them by the priests, and that Christ is bodily under the form of bread and wine, and is therefore to be worshiped in them. And thus the Mass at bottom is nothing else than a denial of the one sacrifice and suffering of Jesus Christ,[5] and an accursed idolatry.

[1] **Heb. 7:27.** Who does not need daily, as those high priests, to offer up sacrifices, first for His own sins and then for the people's, for this He did once for all when He offered up Himself.

Heb. 9:12, 25–28. Not with the blood of goats and calves, but with His own blood He entered the Most Holy Place once for all, having obtained eternal redemption. ... Nor that He should offer Himself often, as the high priest enters the Most Holy Place every year with blood of another—He then would have had to suffer often since the foundation of the world; but now, once at the end of the ages, He has appeared to put away sin by the sacrifice of Himself. And as it is appointed for men to die once, but after this the judgment, so Christ was offered once to bear the sins of many. To those who eagerly wait for Him He will appear a second time, apart from sin, for salvation.

Heb. 10:10, 12, 14. By that will we have been sanctified through the offering of the body of Jesus Christ once for all. ... But this Man, after He had offered one sacrifice for sins forever, sat down at the right hand of God. ... For by one offering He has perfected forever those who are being sanctified.

Jn. 19:30. So when Jesus had received the sour wine, He said, "It is finished!" And bowing His head, He gave up His spirit.

[2] **1 Cor. 6:17.** But he who is joined to the Lord is one spirit with Him.

[3] **Heb. 1:3.** Who, being the brightness of His glory and the express image of His person, and upholding all things by the word of His power, when He had by Himself purged our sins, sat down at the right hand of the Majesty on high.

Heb. 8:1. Now this is the main point of the things we are saying: we have such a High Priest, who is seated at the right hand of the throne of the Majesty in the heavens.

[4] **Jn. 4:21–24.** Jesus said to her, "Woman, believe Me, the hour is coming when you will neither on this mountain, nor in Jerusalem, worship the Father. You worship what you do not know; we know what we worship, for salvation is of the Jews. But the hour is coming, and now is, when the true worshipers will worship the Father in spirit and truth; for the Father is seeking such to worship Him. God is Spirit, and those who worship Him must worship in spirit and truth."

Jn. 20:17. Jesus said to her, "Do not cling to Me, for I have not yet ascended to My Father; but go to My brethren and say to them, 'I am ascending to My Father and your Father, and to My God and your God.'"

Lk. 24:52. And they worshiped Him, and returned to Jerusalem with great joy.

Acts 7:55. But he, being full of the Holy Spirit, gazed into heaven and saw the glory of God, and Jesus standing at the right hand of God.

Col. 3:1. If then you were raised with Christ, seek those things which are above, where Christ is, sitting at the right hand of God.

Phil. 3:20–21. For our citizenship is in heaven, from which we also eagerly wait for the Savior, the Lord Jesus Christ, who will transform our lowly body that it may be conformed to His glorious body, according to the working by which He is able even to subdue all things to Himself.

1 Thess. 1:9–10. For they themselves declare concerning us what manner of entry we had to you, and how you turned to God from idols to serve the living and true God, and to wait for His Son from heaven, whom He raised from the dead, even Jesus who delivers us from the wrath to come.

[5] *See Hebrews chapters 9 and 10.*

✣ **Matt. 4:10.** Then Jesus said to him, "Away with you, Satan! For it is written, 'You shall worship the LORD your God, and Him only you shall serve.'"

81. Who are to come to the table of the Lord?

Those who are displeased with themselves for their sins, yet trust that these are forgiven them, and that their remaining infirmity is covered by the suffering and death of Christ who also desire more and more to strengthen their faith and to amend their life. But the unrepentant and hypocrites eat and drink judgment to themselves.[1]

[1] **1 Cor. 10:19–22.** What am I saying then? That an idol is anything, or what is offered to idols is anything? Rather, that the things which the Gentiles sacrifice they sacrifice to demons and not to God, and I do not want you to

have fellowship with demons. You cannot drink the cup of the Lord and the cup of demons; you cannot partake of the Lord's table and of the table of demons. Or do we provoke the Lord to jealousy? Are we stronger than He?

1 Cor. 11:28–29. But let a man examine himself, and so let him eat of the bread and drink of the cup. For he who eats and drinks in an unworthy manner eats and drinks judgment to himself, not discerning the Lord's body.

✛ **Ps. 51:3.** For I acknowledge my transgressions, and my sin is always before me.

✛ **Jn. 7:37–38.** On the last day, that great day of the feast, Jesus stood and cried out, saying, "If anyone thirsts, let him come to Me and drink. He who believes in Me, as the Scripture has said, out of his heart will flow rivers of living water."

✛ **Ps. 103:1–4.** Bless the LORD, O my soul; and all that is within me, bless His holy name! Bless the LORD, O my soul, and forget not all His benefits: who forgives all your iniquities, who heals all your diseases, who redeems your life from destruction, who crowns you with lovingkindness and tender mercies.

✛ **Matt. 5:6.** Blessed are those who hunger and thirst for righteousness, for they shall be filled.

82. Are they, then, also to be admitted to this Supper who show themselves by their confession and life to be unbelieving and ungodly?

No, for thereby the covenant of God is profaned and His wrath provoked against the whole congregation;[1] therefore, the Christian Church is bound, according to the order of Christ and His Apostles, to exclude such persons by the Office of the Keys until they amend their lives.

[1] **1 Cor. 11:20, 34a.** Therefore when you come together in one place, it is not to eat the Lord's Supper. ... But if anyone is hungry, let him eat at home.

Isa. 1:11–15. "To what purpose is the multitude of your sacrifices to Me?" says the LORD. "I have had enough of burnt offerings of rams and the fat of fed cattle. I do not delight in the blood of bulls, or of lambs or goats. When you come to appear before Me, who has required this from your hand, to trample My courts? Bring no more futile sacrifices; incense is an abomination to Me. The New Moons, the Sabbaths, and the calling of assemblies—I cannot endure iniquity and the sacred meeting. Your New Moons and your appointed feasts My soul hates; they are a trouble to Me, I am weary of bearing them. When you spread out your hands, I will hide My eyes from you; even though you make many prayers, I will not hear. Your hands are full of blood."

Isa. 66:3. He who kills a bull is as if he slays a man; He who sacrifices a lamb, as if he breaks a dog's neck; He who offers a grain offering, as if he offers swine's blood; He who burns incense, as if he blesses an idol. Just as they have chosen their own ways, and their soul delights in their abominations.

Jer. 7:21–23. Thus says the LORD of hosts, the God of Israel: "Add your burnt offerings to your sacrifices and eat meat. For I did not speak to your fathers, or command them in the day that I brought them out of the land of Egypt, concerning burnt offerings or sacrifices. But this is what I commanded them, saying, 'Obey My voice, and I will be your God, and you shall be My people. And walk in all the ways that I have commanded you, that it may be well with you.'"

Psalm 50:16–17. But to the wicked God says: "What right have you to declare My statutes, or take My covenant in your mouth, seeing you hate instruction and cast My words behind you?"

✣ **Matt. 7:6.** Do not give what is holy to the dogs; nor cast your pearls before swine, lest they trample them under their feet, and turn and tear you in pieces.

✣ **1 Cor. 11:30–32.** For this reason many are weak and sick among you, and many sleep. For if we would judge ourselves, we would not be judged. But when we are judged, we are chastened by the Lord, that we may not be condemned with the world.

✣ **Tit. 3:10–11.** Reject a divisive man after the first and second admonition, knowing that such a person is warped and sinning, being self-condemned.

✣ **2 Thess. 3:6.** But we command you, brethren, in the name of our Lord Jesus Christ, that you withdraw from every brother who walks disorderly and not according to the tradition which he received from us.

LORD'S DAY 31

83. What is the Office of the Keys?

The preaching of the Holy Gospel and Christian discipline; by these two the kingdom of heaven is opened to believers and shut against unbelievers.[1]

[1] **Matt. 16:18–19.** And I also say to you that you are Peter, and on this rock I will build My church, and the gates of Hades shall not prevail against it.

And I will give you the keys of the kingdom of heaven, and whatever you bind on earth will be bound in heaven, and whatever you loose on earth will be loosed in heaven.

Matt. 18:18. Assuredly, I say to you, whatever you bind on earth will be bound in heaven, and whatever you loose on earth will be loosed in heaven.

✢ **Jn. 20:23.** If you forgive the sins of any, they are forgiven them; if you retain the sins of any, they are retained.

✢ **Lk. 24:46–47.** Then He said to them, "Thus it is written, and thus it was necessary for the Christ to suffer and to rise from the dead the third day, and that repentance and remission of sins should be preached in His name to all nations, beginning at Jerusalem."

✢ **1 Cor. 1:23–24.** But we preach Christ crucified, to the Jews a stumbling block and to the Greeks foolishness, but to those who are called, both Jews and Greeks, Christ the power of God and the wisdom of God.

84. How is the kingdom of heaven opened and shut by the preaching of the Holy Gospel?

In this way: that, according to the command of Christ, it is proclaimed and openly witnessed to believers, one and all, that as often as they accept with true faith the promise of the Gospel, all their sins are really forgiven them of God for the sake of Christ's merits; and on the contrary, to all unbelievers and hypocrites, that the wrath of God and eternal condemnation abide on them so long as they are not converted.[1] According to this testimony of the Gospel, God will judge men both in this life and in that which is to come.

[1] **Jn. 20:21–23.** So Jesus said to them again, "Peace to you! As the Father has sent Me, I also send you." And when He had said this, He breathed on them, and said to them, "Receive the Holy Spirit. If you forgive the sins of any, they are forgiven them; if you retain the sins of any, they are retained."

✢ **Acts 10:43.** To Him all the prophets witness that, through His name, whoever believes in Him will receive remission of sins.

✢ **Isa. 58:1.** Cry aloud, spare not; Lift up your voice like a trumpet; tell My people their transgression, and the house of Jacob their sins.

✢ **2 Cor. 2:15–16.** For we are to God the fragrance of Christ among those who are being saved and among those who are perishing. To the one we are the aroma of death leading to death, and to the other the aroma of life leading to life. And who is sufficient for these things?

✢ **Jn. 8:24.** Therefore I said to you that you will die in your sins; for if you do not believe that I am He, you will die in your sins.

85. How is the kingdom of heaven shut and opened by Christian discipline?

In this way: that, according to the command of Christ, if any under the Christian name show themselves unsound either in doctrine or in life, and after several brotherly admonitions do not turn from their errors or evil ways, they are complained of to the Church or to its proper officers; and, if they neglect to hear them also, are by them denied the holy sacraments and thereby excluded from the Christian communion, and by God Himself from the kingdom of Christ; and if they promise and show real amendment, they are again received as members of Christ and His Church.[1]

[1] **Matt. 18:15–18.** Moreover if your brother sins against you, go and tell him his fault between you and him alone. If he hears you, you have gained your brother. But if he will not hear, take with you one or two more, that "by the mouth of two or three witnesses every word may be established." And if he refuses to hear them, tell it to the church. But if he refuses even to hear the church, let him be to you like a heathen and a tax collector. Assuredly, I say to you, whatever you bind on earth will be bound in heaven, and whatever you loose on earth will be loosed in heaven.

1 Cor. 5:3–5, 11. For I indeed, as absent in body but present in spirit, have already judged (as though I were present) him who has so done this deed. In the name of our Lord Jesus Christ, when you are gathered together, along with my spirit, with the power of our Lord Jesus Christ, deliver such a one to Satan for the destruction of the flesh, that his spirit may be saved in the day of the Lord Jesus. ... But now I have written to you not to keep company with anyone named a brother, who is sexually immoral, or covetous, or an idolater, or a reviler, or a drunkard, or an extortioner not even to eat with such a person.

2 Thess. 3:14–15. And if anyone does not obey our word in this epistle, note that person and do not keep company with him, that he may be ashamed. Yet do not count him as an enemy, but admonish him as a brother.

2 Jn. 10–11. If anyone comes to you and does not bring this doctrine, do not receive him into your house nor greet him; for he who greets him shares in his evil deeds.

Third Part: Our Thankfulness

LORD'S DAY 32

86. Since, then, we are redeemed from our misery by grace through Christ, without any merit of ours, why must we do good works?

Because Christ, having redeemed us by His blood, also renews us by His Holy Spirit after His own image, that with our whole life we show ourselves thankful to God for His blessing,[1] and that He be glorified through us;[2] then also, that we ourselves may be assured of our faith by the fruits thereof;[3] and by our Godly walk win also others to Christ.[4]

[1] **Rom. 6:13.** And do not present your members as instruments of unrighteousness to sin, but present yourselves to God as being alive from the dead, and your members as instruments of righteousness to God.

Rom. 12:1–2. I beseech you therefore, brethren, by the mercies of God, that you present your bodies a living sacrifice, holy, acceptable to God, which is your reasonable service. And do not be conformed to this world, but be transformed by the renewing of your mind, that you may prove what is that good and acceptable and perfect will of God.

1 Pet. 2:5, 9–10. You also, as living stones, are being built up a spiritual house, a holy priesthood, to offer up spiritual sacrifices acceptable to God through Jesus Christ. ... But you are a chosen generation, a royal priesthood, a holy nation, His own special people, that you may proclaim the praises of Him who called you out of darkness into His marvelous light; who once were not a people but are now the people of God, who had not obtained mercy but now have obtained mercy.

1 Cor. 6:20. For you were bought at a price; therefore glorify God in your body and in your spirit, which are God's.

[2] **Matt. 5:16.** Let your light so shine before men, that they may see your good works and glorify your Father in heaven.

1 Pet. 2:12. Having your conduct honorable among the Gentiles, that when they speak against you as evildoers, they may, by your good works which they observe, glorify God in the day of visitation.

[3] **Matt. 7:17–18.** Even so, every good tree bears good fruit, but a bad tree bears bad fruit. A good tree cannot bear bad fruit, nor can a bad tree bear good fruit.

Gal. 5:6, 22–23. For in Christ Jesus neither circumcision nor uncircumcision avails anything, but faith working through love. ... But the fruit of the Spirit is love, joy, peace, longsuffering, kindness, goodness, faithfulness, gentleness, self-control. Against such there is no law.

[4] **Rom. 14:19.** Therefore let us pursue the things which make for peace and the things by which one may edify another.

1 Pet. 3:1–2. Wives, likewise, be submissive to your own husbands, that even if some do not obey the word, they, without a word, may be won by the conduct of their wives, when they observe your chaste conduct accompanied by fear.

✢ **2 Pet. 1:10.** Therefore, brethren, be even more diligent to make your call and election sure, for if you do these things you will never stumble.

87. Can they, then, not be saved who do not turn to God from their unthankful, unrepentant life?

By no means, for, as Scripture says, no unchaste person, idolater, adulterer, thief, covetous man, drunkard, slanderer, robber, or the like shall inherit the kingdom of God.[1]

[1] **1 Cor. 6:9–10.** Do you not know that the unrighteous will not inherit the kingdom of God? Do not be deceived. Neither fornicators, nor idolaters, nor adulterers, nor homosexuals, nor sodomites, nor thieves, nor covetous, nor drunkards, nor revilers, nor extortioners will inherit the kingdom of God.

Eph. 5:5–6. For this you know, that no fornicator, unclean person, nor covetous man, who is an idolater, has any inheritance in the kingdom of Christ and God. Let no one deceive you with empty words, for because of these things the wrath of God comes upon the sons of disobedience.

1 Jn. 3:14–15. We know that we have passed from death to life, because we love the brethren. He who does not love his brother abides in death. Whoever hates his brother is a murderer, and you know that no murderer has eternal life abiding in him.

LORD'S DAY 33

88. In how many things does true repentance or conversion consist?

In two things: the dying of the old man,[1] and the making alive of the new.

[1] **Rom. 6:4–6.** Therefore we were buried with Him through baptism into death, that just as Christ was raised from the dead by the glory of the Father, even so we also should walk in newness of life. For if we have been united together in the likeness of His death, certainly we also shall be in the likeness of His resurrection, knowing this, that our old man was crucified with Him, that the body of sin might be done away with, that we should no longer be slaves of sin.

Eph. 4:22–24. That you put off, concerning your former conduct, the old man which grows corrupt according to the deceitful lusts, and be renewed in the spirit of your mind, and that you put on the new man which was created according to God, in true righteousness and holiness.

Col. 3:5–10. Therefore put to death your members which are on the earth: fornication, uncleanness, passion, evil desire, and covetousness, which is idolatry. Because of these things the wrath of God is coming upon the sons of disobedience, in which you yourselves once walked when you lived in them. But now you yourselves are to put off all these: anger, wrath, malice, blasphemy, filthy language out of your mouth. Do not lie to one another, since you have put off the old man with his deeds, and have put on the new man who is renewed in knowledge according to the image of Him who created him.

1 Cor. 5:7. Therefore purge out the old leaven, that you may be a new lump, since you truly are unleavened. For indeed Christ, our Passover, was sacrificed for us.

89. What is the dying of the old man?

Heartfelt sorrow for sin, causing us to hate and turn from it always more and more.[1]

[1] **Rom. 8:13.** For if you live according to the flesh you will die; but if by the Spirit you put to death the deeds of the body, you will live.

Joel 2:13. So rend your heart, and not your garments; Return to the LORD your God, for He is gracious and merciful, slow to anger, and of great kindness; and He relents from doing harm.

90. What is the making alive of the new man?

Heartfelt joy in God through Christ,[1] causing us to take delight in living according to the will of God in all good works.[2]

[1] **Rom. 5:1.** Therefore, having been justified by faith, we have peace with God through our Lord Jesus Christ.

Rom. 14:17. For the kingdom of God is not eating and drinking, but righteousness and peace and joy in the Holy Spirit.

Isa. 57:15. For thus says the High and Lofty One who inhabits eternity, whose name is Holy: "I dwell in the high and holy place, with him who has a contrite and humble spirit, to revive the spirit of the humble, and to revive the heart of the contrite ones."

[2] **Rom. 8:10–11.** And if Christ is in you, the body is dead because of sin, but the Spirit is life because of righteousness. But if the Spirit of Him who raised Jesus from the dead dwells in you, He who raised Christ from the dead will also give life to your mortal bodies through His Spirit who dwells in you.

Gal. 2:20. I have been crucified with Christ; it is no longer I who live, but Christ lives in me; and the life which I now live in the flesh I live by faith in the Son of God, who loved me and gave Himself for me.

✢ **Rom. 7:22.** For I delight in the law of God according to the inward man.

91. What are good works?

Those only which proceed from true faith,[1] and are done according to the law of God,[2] unto His glory,[3] and not such as rest on our own opinion[4] or the commandments of men.[5]

[1] **Rom. 14:23.** But he who doubts is condemned if he eats, because he does not eat from faith; for whatever is not from faith is sin.

[2] **1 Sam. 15:22.** So Samuel said: "Has the LORD as great delight in burnt offerings and sacrifices, as in obeying the voice of the LORD? Behold, to obey is better than sacrifice, and to heed than the fat of rams."

Eph. 2:10. For we are His workmanship, created in Christ Jesus for good works, which God prepared beforehand that we should walk in them.

[3] **1 Cor. 10:31.** Therefore, whether you eat or drink, or whatever you do, do all to the glory of God.

[4] **Deut. 12:32.** Whatever I command you, be careful to observe it; you shall not add to it nor take away from it.

Ezek. 20:18, 20. But I said to their children in the wilderness, "Do not walk in the statutes of your fathers, nor observe their judgments, nor defile yourselves with their idols. ... Hallow My Sabbaths, and they will be a sign between Me and you, that you may know that I am the LORD your God."

Isa. 29:13. Therefore the LORD said: "Inasmuch as these people draw near with their mouths and honor Me with their lips, but have removed their hearts far from Me, and their fear toward Me is taught by the commandment of men."

[5] Matt. 15:9. And in vain they worship Me, teaching as doctrines the commandments of men.

✣ Num. 15:39. And you shall have the tassel, that you may look upon it and remember all the commandments of the LORD and do them, and that you may not follow the harlotry to which your own heart and your own eyes are inclined.

The Law of God

92. What is the law of God?

And God spoke all these words, saying:

First Commandment

I am the LORD your God, who brought you out of the land of Egypt, out of the house of bondage. You shall have no other gods before Me.

Second Commandment

You shall not make for yourself a carved image—any likeness of anything that is in heaven above, or that is in the earth beneath, or that is in the water under the earth; you shall not bow down to them nor serve them. For I, the LORD your God, am a jealous God, visiting the iniquity of the fathers upon the children to the third and fourth generations of those who hate Me, but showing mercy to thousands, to those who love Me and keep My commandments.

Third Commandment

You shall not take the name of the LORD your God in vain, for the LORD will not hold him guiltless who takes His name in vain.

Fourth Commandment

Remember the Sabbath day, to keep it holy. Six days you shall labor and do all your work, but the seventh day is the Sabbath of the LORD your God. In it you shall do no work: you, nor your son, nor your daughter, nor your male servant, nor your female servant, nor your cattle, nor your stranger who is within your gates. For in six days the LORD made the heavens and the earth, the sea, and all that is in them, and rested the seventh day. Therefore the LORD blessed the Sabbath day and hallowed it.

Fifth Commandment

Honor your father and your mother, that your days may be long upon the land which the LORD your God is giving you.

Sixth Commandment

You shall not murder.

Seventh Commandment

You shall not commit adultery.

Eighth Commandment

You shall not steal.

Ninth Commandment

You shall not bear false witness against your neighbor.

Tenth Commandment

You shall not covet your neighbor's house, you shall not covet your neighbor's wife, nor his male servant, nor his female servant, nor his ox, nor his donkey, nor anything that is your neighbor's.[1]

[1] *See Exodus 20 & Deuteronomy 5.*

✣ **Matt. 5:17–19.** Do not think that I came to destroy the Law or the Prophets. I did not come to destroy but to fulfill. For assuredly, I say to you, till heaven and earth pass away, one jot or one tittle will by no means pass from the law till all is fulfilled. Whoever therefore breaks one of the least of these commandments, and teaches men so, shall be called least in the kingdom of heaven; but whoever does and teaches them, he shall be called great in the kingdom of heaven.

✣ **Rom. 10:5.** For Moses writes about the righteousness which is of the law, "The man who does those things shall live by them."

✣ **Rom. 3:31.** Do we then make void the law through faith? Certainly not! On the contrary, we establish the law.

✣ **Ps. 119:9.** How can a young man cleanse his way? By taking heed according to Your word.

LORD'S DAY 34

93. How are these commandments divided?

Into two tables:[1] the *first* of which teaches, in four commandments, what duties we owe to God; the *second*, in six, what duties we owe to our neighbor.[2]

[1] **Ex. 34:28.** So he was there with the LORD forty days and forty nights; he neither ate bread nor drank water. And He wrote on the tablets the words of the covenant, the Ten Commandments.

Deut. 4:13. So He declared to you His covenant which He commanded you to perform, the Ten Commandments; and He wrote them on two tablets of stone.

[2] **Matt. 22:37–40.** Jesus said to him, "You shall love the LORD your God with all your heart, with all your soul, and with all your mind. This is the first and great commandment. And the second is like it: you shall love your neighbor as yourself. On these two commandments hang all the Law and the Prophets."

94. What does God require in the first commandment?

That, on peril of my soul's salvation, I avoid and flee all idolatry,[1] sorcery, enchantments,[2] invocation of saints or of other creatures;[3] and that I rightly acknowledge the only true God,[4] trust in Him alone,[5] with all humility[6] and patience[7] expect all good from Him only,[8] and love,[9] fear,[10] and honor[11] Him with my whole heart; so as rather to renounce all creatures than to do the least thing against His will.[12]

[1] **1 Cor. 10:7, 14.** And do not become idolaters as were some of them. As it is written, "The people sat down to eat and drink, and rose up to play." ... Therefore, my beloved, flee from idolatry.

[2] **Lev. 19:31.** Give no regard to mediums and familiar spirits; do not seek after them, to be defiled by them: I am the LORD your God.

Deut. 18:10–12. There shall not be found among you anyone who makes his son or his daughter pass through the fire, or one who practices witchcraft, or a soothsayer, or one who interprets omens, or a sorcerer, or one who conjures spells, or a medium, or a spiritist, or one who calls up the dead. For all who do these things are an abomination to the LORD, and because of these abominations the LORD your God drives them out from before you.

[3] **Matt. 4:10.** Then Jesus said to him, "Away with you, Satan! For it is written, 'You shall worship the LORD your God, and Him only you shall serve.'"

Rev. 19:10. And I fell at his feet to worship him. But he said to me, "See that you do not do that! I am your fellow servant, and of your brethren who have the testimony of Jesus. Worship God! For the testimony of Jesus is the spirit of prophecy."

Rev. 22:8–9. Now I, John, saw and heard these things. And when I heard and saw, I fell down to worship before the feet of the angel who showed me these things. Then he said to me, "See that you do not do that. For I am your fellow servant, and of your brethren the prophets, and of those who keep the words of this book. Worship God."

[4] **Jn. 17:3.** And this is eternal life, that they may know You, the only true God, and Jesus Christ whom You have sent.

[5] **Jer. 17:5.** Thus says the LORD, "Cursed is the man who trusts in man and makes flesh his strength, whose heart departs from the LORD."

[6] **1 Pet. 5:5–6.** Likewise you younger people, submit yourselves to your elders. Yes, all of you be submissive to one another, and be clothed with humility, for "God resists the proud, but gives grace to the humble." Therefore humble yourselves under the mighty hand of God, that He may exalt you in due time.

[7] **Heb. 10:36.** For you have need of endurance, so that after you have done the will of God, you may receive the promise.

Col. 1:10b–11. And increasing in the knowledge of God; strengthened with all might, according to His glorious power, for all patience and longsuffering with joy.

Rom. 5:3–4. And not only that, but we also glory in tribulations, knowing that tribulation produces perseverance; and perseverance, character; and character, hope.

1 Cor. 10:10. Nor complain, as some of them also complained, and were destroyed by the destroyer.

[8] **Ps. 104:27–30.** These all wait for You, that You may give them their food in due season. What You give them they gather in; You open Your hand, they are filled with good. You hide Your face, they are troubled; You take away their breath, they die and return to their dust. You send forth Your Spirit, they are created; and You renew the face of the earth.

Isa. 45:6b–7. I am the LORD, and there is no other; I form the light and create darkness, I make peace and create calamity; I, the LORD, do all these things.

Jas. 1:17. Every good gift and every perfect gift is from above, and comes down from the Father of lights, with whom there is no variation or shadow of turning.

[9] **Deut. 6:5.** You shall love the LORD your God with all your heart, with all your soul, and with all your strength.

[10] **Deut. 6:2.** That you may fear the LORD your God, to keep all His statutes and His commandments which I command you, you and your son and your grandson, all the days of your life, and that your days may be prolonged.

Ps. 111:10. The fear of the LORD is the beginning of wisdom; a good understanding have all those who do His commandments. His praise endures forever.

Prov. 9:10. The fear of the LORD is the beginning of wisdom, and the knowledge of the Holy One is understanding.

Matt. 10:28. And do not fear those who kill the body but cannot kill the soul. But rather fear Him who is able to destroy both soul and body in hell.

[11] **Deut. 10:20.** You shall fear the LORD your God; you shall serve Him, and to Him you shall hold fast, and take oaths in His name.

[12] **Matt. 5:29–30.** If your right eye causes you to sin, pluck it out and cast it from you; for it is more profitable for you that one of your members perish, than for your whole body to be cast into hell. And if your right hand causes you to sin, cut it off and cast it from you; for it is more profitable for you that one of your members perish, than for your whole body to be cast into hell.

Matt. 10:37. He who loves father or mother more than Me is not worthy of Me. And he who loves son or daughter more than Me is not worthy of Me.

Acts 5:29. But Peter and the other apostles answered and said: "We ought to obey God rather than men."

95. What is idolatry?

Idolatry is to conceive or have something else in which to place our trust instead of, or besides, the one true God who has revealed Himself in His Word.[1]

[1] **Eph. 5:5.** For this you know, that no fornicator, unclean person, nor covetous man, who is an idolater, has any inheritance in the kingdom of Christ and God.

Phil. 3:19. Whose end is destruction, whose God is their belly, and whose glory is in their shame—who set their mind on earthly things.

Eph. 2:12. That at that time you were without Christ, being aliens from the commonwealth of Israel and strangers from the covenants of promise, having no hope and without God in the world.

Jn. 2:23. Now when He was in Jerusalem at the Passover, during the feast, many believed in His name when they saw the signs which He did.

2 Jn. 9. Whoever transgresses and does not abide in the doctrine of Christ does not have God. He who abides in the doctrine of Christ has both the Father and the Son.

Jn. 5:23. That all should honor the Son just as they honor the Father. He who does not honor the Son does not honor the Father who sent Him.

✤ **Ps. 81:8–9.** Hear, O My people, and I will admonish you! O Israel, if you will listen to Me! There shall be no foreign god among you; nor shall you worship any foreign god.

✤ **Matt. 6:24.** No one can serve two masters; for either he will hate the one and love the other, or else he will be loyal to the one and despise the other. You cannot serve God and mammon.

✤ **Ps. 62:5–7.** My soul, wait silently for God alone, for my expectation is from Him. He only is my rock and my salvation; He is my defense; I shall not be moved. In God is my salvation and my glory; the rock of my strength, and my refuge, is in God.

✤ **Ps. 73:25–26.** Whom have I in heaven but You? And there is none upon earth that I desire besides You. My flesh and my heart fail; but God is the strength of my heart and my portion forever.

Lord's Day 35

96. What does God require in the second commandment?

That we in no way make any image of God,[1] nor worship Him in any other way than He has commanded us in His Word.[2]

[1] **Deut. 4:15–19.** Take careful heed to yourselves, for you saw no form when the Lord spoke to you at Horeb out of the midst of the fire, lest you act corruptly and make for yourselves a carved image in the form of any figure: the likeness of male or female, the likeness of any animal that is on the earth or the likeness of any winged bird that flies in the air, the likeness of anything that creeps on the ground or the likeness of any fish that is in the water beneath the earth. And take heed, lest you lift your eyes to heaven, and when you see the sun, the moon, and the stars, all the host of heaven,

you feel driven to worship them and serve them, which the LORD your God has given to all the peoples under the whole heaven as a heritage.

Isa. 40:18, 25. "To whom then will you liken God? Or what likeness will you compare to Him? ... To whom then will you liken Me, or to whom shall I be equal?" says the Holy One.

Rom. 1:22–24. Professing to be wise, they became fools, and changed the glory of the incorruptible God into an image made like corruptible man— and birds and four-footed animals and creeping things. Therefore God also gave them up to uncleanness, in the lusts of their hearts, to dishonor their bodies among themselves.

Acts 17:29. Therefore, since we are the offspring of God, we ought not to think that the Divine Nature is like gold or silver or stone, something shaped by art and man's devising.

[2] **1 Sam. 15:23.** For rebellion is as the sin of witchcraft, and stubbornness is as iniquity and idolatry. Because you have rejected the word of the LORD, He also has rejected you from being king.

Deut. 12:30–32. Take heed to yourself that you are not ensnared to follow them, after they are destroyed from before you, and that you do not inquire after their gods, saying, "How did these nations serve their gods? I also will do likewise." You shall not worship the LORD your God in that way; for every abomination to the LORD which He hates they have done to their gods; for they burn even their sons and daughters in the fire to their gods. Whatever I command you, be careful to observe it; you shall not add to it nor take away from it.

Matt. 15:9. And in vain they worship Me, teaching as doctrines the commandments of men.

✢ **Deut. 4:23–24.** Take heed to yourselves, lest you forget the covenant of the LORD your God which He made with you, and make for yourselves a carved image in the form of anything which the LORD your God has forbidden you. For the LORD your God is a consuming fire, a jealous God.

✢ **Jn. 4:24.** God is Spirit, and those who worship Him must worship in spirit and truth.

97. May we not make any image at all?

God may not and cannot be imaged in any way; as for creatures, though they may indeed be imaged, yet God forbids the making or keeping of any likeness of them, either to worship them or to serve God by them.[1]

[1] **Ex. 23:24–25.** You shall not bow down to their gods, nor serve them, nor do according to their works; but you shall utterly overthrow them and completely break down their sacred pillars. So you shall serve the LORD your God, and He will bless your bread and your water. And I will take sickness away from the midst of you.

Ex. 34:13–14. But you shall destroy their altars, break their sacred pillars, and cut down their wooden images (for you shall worship no other god, for the LORD, whose name is Jealous, is a jealous God).

Deut. 7:5. But thus you shall deal with them: you shall destroy their altars, and break down their sacred pillars, and cut down their wooden images, and burn their carved images with fire.

Deut. 12:3. And you shall destroy their altars, break their sacred pillars, and burn their wooden images with fire; you shall cut down the carved images of their gods and destroy their names from that place.

Deut. 16:22. You shall not set up a sacred pillar, which the LORD your God hates.

2 Kgs. 18:4. He removed the high places and broke the sacred pillars, cut down the wooden image and broke in pieces the bronze serpent that Moses had made; for until those days the children of Israel burned incense to it, and called it Nehushtan.

✢ **Jn. 1:18.** No one has seen God at any time. The only begotten Son, who is in the bosom of the Father, He has declared Him.

98. But may not pictures be tolerated in churches as books for the people?

No, for we should not be wiser than God, who will not have His people taught by dumb idols,[1] but by the lively preaching of His Word.[2]

[1] **Jer. 10:8.** But they are altogether dull-hearted and foolish; a wooden idol is a worthless doctrine.

Hab. 2:18–19. What profit is the image, that its maker should carve it, the molded image, a teacher of lies, that the maker of its mold should trust in it, to make mute idols? Woe to him who says to wood, "Awake!" to silent stone, "Arise! It shall teach!" Behold, it is overlaid with gold and silver, yet in it there is no breath at all.

[2] **2 Pet. 1:19.** And so we have the prophetic word confirmed, which you do well to heed as a light that shines in a dark place, until the day dawns and the morning star rises in your hearts.

2 Tim. 3:16–17. All Scripture is given by inspiration of God, and is profitable for doctrine, for reproof, for correction, for instruction in righteousness, that the man of God may be complete, thoroughly equipped for every good work.

✢ **Rom. 10:17.** So then faith comes by hearing, and hearing by the word of God.

LORD'S DAY 36

99. What is required in the third commandment?

That we must not by cursing,[1] or by false swearing,[2] nor yet by unnecessary oaths,[3] profane or abuse the name of God; nor even by our silence and connivance be partakers of these horrible sins in others; and in summary, that we use the holy name of God in no other way than with fear and reverence,[4] so that He may be rightly confessed[5] and worshiped[6] by us, and be glorified in all our words and works.[7]

[1] **Lev. 24:10–16.** Now the son of an Israelite woman, whose father was an Egyptian, went out among the children of Israel; and this Israelite woman's son and a man of Israel fought each other in the camp. And the Israelite woman's son blasphemed the name of the LORD and cursed; and so they brought him to Moses. (His mother's name was Shelomith the daughter of Dibri, of the tribe of Dan.) Then they put him in custody, that the mind of the LORD might be shown to them. And the LORD spoke to Moses, saying, "Take outside the camp him who has cursed; then let all who heard him lay their hands on his head, and let all the congregation stone him. Then you shall speak to the children of Israel, saying: 'Whoever curses his God shall bear his sin. And whoever blasphemes the name of the LORD shall surely be put to death. All the congregation shall certainly stone him, the stranger as well as him who is born in the land. When he blasphemes the name of the LORD, he shall be put to death.'"

[2] **Lev. 19:12.** And you shall not swear by My name falsely, nor shall you profane the name of your God: I am the LORD.

[3] **Matt. 5:37.** But let your 'Yes' be 'Yes,' and your 'No,' 'No.' For whatever is more than these is from the evil one.

Jas. 5:12. But above all, my brethren, do not swear, either by heaven or by earth or with any other oath. But let your 'Yes' be 'Yes,' and your 'No,' 'No,' lest you fall into judgment.

[4] **Isa. 45:23.** I have sworn by Myself; the word has gone out of My mouth in righteousness, and shall not return, that to Me every knee shall bow, every tongue shall take an oath.

[5] **Matt. 10:32.** Therefore whoever confesses Me before men, him I will also confess before My Father who is in heaven.

[6] **1 Tim. 2:8.** I desire therefore that the men pray everywhere, lifting up holy hands, without wrath and doubting.

[7] **Rom. 2:24.** For "the name of God is blasphemed among the Gentiles because of you," as it is written.

1 Tim. 6:1. Let as many bondservants as are under the yoke count their own masters worthy of all honor, so that the name of God and His doctrine may not be blasphemed.

Col. 3:16–17. Let the word of Christ dwell in you richly in all wisdom, teaching and admonishing one another in psalms and hymns and spiritual songs, singing with grace in your hearts to the Lord. And whatever you do in word or deed, do all in the name of the Lord Jesus, giving thanks to God the Father through Him.

✢ **1 Pet. 3:15.** But sanctify the Lord God in your hearts, and always be ready to give a defense to everyone who asks you a reason for the hope that is in you, with meekness and fear.

100. Is the profaning of God's name, by swearing and cursing, so grievous a sin that His wrath is kindled against those also who do not help as much as they can to hinder and forbid it?

Yes, truly,[1] for no sin is greater and more provoking to God than the profaning of His name; wherefore He even commanded it to be punished with death.[2]

[1] **Lev. 5:1.** If a person sins in hearing the utterance of an oath, and is a witness, whether he has seen or known of the matter—if he does not tell it, he bears guilt.

[2] **Lev. 24:15–16.** Then you shall speak to the children of Israel, saying: "Whoever curses his God shall bear his sin. And whoever blasphemes the name of the LORD shall surely be put to death. All the congregation shall certainly stone him, the stranger as well as him who is born in the land. When he blasphemes the name of the LORD, he shall be put to death."

✢ **Lev. 19:12.** And you shall not swear by My name falsely, nor shall you profane the name of your God: I am the LORD.

✢ **Prov. 29:24–25.** Whoever is a partner with a thief hates his own life; he swears to tell the truth, but reveals nothing. The fear of man brings a snare, but whoever trusts in the LORD shall be safe.

LORD'S DAY 37

101. But may we swear reverently by the name of God?

Yes, when the magistrate requires it, or when it may be needful otherwise, to maintain and promote fidelity and truth to the glory of God and our neighbor's good; for such an oath is grounded in God's Word,[1] and therefore was rightly used by the saints in the Old and New Testaments.[2]

[1] **Deut. 10:20.** You shall fear the LORD your God; you shall serve Him, and to Him you shall hold fast, and take oaths in His name.

Isa. 48:1. Hear this, O house of Jacob, who are called by the name of Israel, and have come forth from the wellsprings of Judah; who swear by the name of the LORD, and make mention of the God of Israel, but not in truth or in righteousness.

Heb. 6:16. For men indeed swear by the greater, and an oath for confirmation is for them an end of all dispute.

[2] **Gen. 21:24.** And Abraham said, "I will swear."

Gen. 31:53–54. The God of Abraham, the God of Nahor, and the God of their father judge between us. And Jacob swore by the Fear of his father Isaac. Then Jacob offered a sacrifice on the mountain, and called his brethren to eat bread. And they ate bread and stayed all night on the mountain.

Josh. 9:15, 19. So Joshua made peace with them, and made a covenant with them to let them live; and the rulers of the congregation swore to them. ... Then all the rulers said to all the congregation, "We have sworn to them by the LORD God of Israel; now therefore, we may not touch them."

1 Sam. 24:22. So David swore to Saul. And Saul went home, but David and his men went up to the stronghold.

1 Kgs. 1:29. And the king took an oath and said, "As the LORD lives, who has redeemed my life from every distress."

Rom. 1:9. For God is my witness, whom I serve with my spirit in the gospel of His Son, that without ceasing I make mention of you always in my prayers.

102. May we swear by "the saints" or by any other creatures?

No, for a lawful oath is a calling upon God, that He, as the only searcher of hearts, may bear witness to the truth, and punish me if I swear falsely;[1] which honor is due to no creature.[2]

[1] **2 Cor. 1:23.** Moreover I call God as witness against my soul, that to spare you I came no more to Corinth.

[2] **Matt. 5:34–36.** But I say to you, do not swear at all: neither by heaven, for it is God's throne; nor by the earth, for it is His footstool; nor by Jerusalem, for it is the city of the great King. Nor shall you swear by your head, because you cannot make one hair white or black.

✣ **Jer. 5:7.** How shall I pardon you for this? Your children have forsaken Me and sworn by those that are not gods. When I had fed them to the full, then they committed adultery and assembled themselves by troops in the harlots' houses.

✣ **Isa. 65:16.** So that he who blesses himself in the earth shall bless himself in the God of truth; and he who swears in the earth shall swear by the God of truth; because the former troubles are forgotten, and because they are hidden from My eyes.

LORD'S DAY 38

103. What does God require in the fourth commandment?

In the *first* place, God wills that the ministry of the Gospel and schools be maintained,[1] and that I, especially on the day of rest, diligently attend church[2] to learn the Word of God,[3] to use the holy sacraments,[4] to call publicly upon the Lord,[5] and to give Christian alms.[6] In the *second* place, that all the days of my life I rest from my evil works, allow the Lord to work in me by His Spirit, and thus begin in this life the everlasting Sabbath.[7]

[1] **Tit. 1:5.** For this reason I left you in Crete, that you should set in order the things that are lacking, and appoint elders in every city as I commanded you.

1 Tim. 3:14–15. These things I write to you, though I hope to come to you shortly; but if I am delayed, I write so that you may know how you ought to conduct yourself in the house of God, which is the church of the living God, the pillar and ground of the truth.

1 Tim. 4:13–14. Till I come, give attention to reading, to exhortation, to doctrine. Do not neglect the gift that is in you, which was given to you by prophecy with the laying on of the hands of the eldership.

1 Tim. 5:17. Let the elders who rule well be counted worthy of double honor, especially those who labor in the word and doctrine.

1 Cor. 9:11, 13–14. If we have sown spiritual things for you, is it a great thing if we reap your material things? ... Do you not know that those who minister the holy things eat of the things of the temple, and those who serve at the altar partake of the offerings of the altar? Even so the Lord has commanded that those who preach the gospel should live from the gospel.

[2] 2 Tim. 2:2. And the things that you have heard from me among many witnesses, commit these to faithful men who will be able to teach others also.

2 Tim. 2:15. ... Be diligent to present yourself approved to God, a worker who does not need to be ashamed, rightly dividing the word of truth.

Ps. 40:10–11. I have not hidden Your righteousness within my heart; I have declared Your faithfulness and Your salvation; I have not concealed Your lovingkindness and Your truth from the great assembly. Do not withhold Your tender mercies from me, O Lord; let Your lovingkindness and Your truth continually preserve me.

Ps. 68:26. Bless God in the congregations, the Lord, from the fountain of Israel.

Acts 2:42, 46. And they continued steadfastly in the apostles' doctrine and fellowship, in the breaking of bread, and in prayers. ... So continuing daily with one accord in the temple, and breaking bread from house to house, they ate their food with gladness and simplicity of heart.

[3] 1 Cor. 14:19, 29, 31. Yet in the church I would rather speak five words with my understanding, that I may teach others also, than ten thousand words in a tongue. ... Let two or three prophets speak, and let the others judge.

[4] 1 Cor. 11:33. Therefore, my brethren, when you come together to eat, wait for one another.

[5] 1 Tim. 2:1–2. Therefore I exhort first of all that supplications, prayers, intercessions, and giving of thanks be made for all men, for kings and all who are in authority, that we may lead a quiet and peaceable life in all godliness and reverence.

1 Tim 2:8–10. I desire therefore that the men pray everywhere, lifting up holy hands, without wrath and doubting; in like manner also, that the women adorn themselves in modest apparel, with propriety and moderation, not with braided hair or gold or pearls or costly clothing, but, which is proper for women professing godliness, with good works.

1 Cor. 14:16. Otherwise, if you bless with the spirit, how will he who occupies the place of the uninformed say "Amen" at your giving of thanks, since he does not understand what you say?

[6] **1 Cor. 16:2.** On the first day of the week let each one of you lay something aside, storing up as he may prosper, that there be no collections when I come.

[7] **Isa. 66:23.** "And it shall come to pass that from one New Moon to another, And from one Sabbath to another, all flesh shall come to worship before Me," says the LORD.

✛ **Gal. 6:6.** Let him who is taught the word share in all good things with him who teaches.

✛ **Acts 20:7.** Now on the first day of the week, when the disciples came together to break bread, Paul, ready to depart the next day, spoke to them and continued his message until midnight.

✛ **Heb. 4:9–10.** There remains therefore a rest for the people of God. For he who has entered His rest has himself also ceased from his works as God did from His.

LORD'S DAY 39

104. What does God require in the fifth commandment?

That I show all honor, love, and faithfulness to my father and mother,[1] and to all in authority over me,[2] submit myself with due obedience to all their good instruction and correction, and also bear patiently with their infirmities, since it is God's will to govern us by their hand.[3]

[1] **Eph. 5:22.** Wives, submit to your own husbands, as to the Lord.

Eph. 6:1–6. Children, obey your parents in the Lord, for this is right. "Honor your father and mother," which is the first commandment with promise: "that it may be well with you and you may live long on the earth." And you, fathers, do not provoke your children to wrath, but bring them up in the training and admonition of the Lord. Bondservants, be obedient to those who are your masters according to the flesh, with fear and trembling, in sincerity of heart, as to Christ; not with eyeservice, as men-pleasers, but as bondservants of Christ, doing the will of God from the heart.

Col. 3:18, 20–24. Wives, submit to your own husbands, as is fitting in the Lord. ... Children, obey your parents in all things, for this is well pleasing to the Lord. Fathers, do not provoke your children, lest they become discouraged. Bondservants, obey in all things your masters according to the flesh, not with eyeservice, as men-pleasers, but in sincerity of heart, fearing God. And whatever you do, do it heartily, as to the Lord and not to men, knowing that from the Lord you will receive the reward of the inheritance; for you serve the Lord Christ.

Prov. 1:8–9. My son, hear the instruction of your father, and do not forsake the law of your mother; for they will be a graceful ornament on your head, and chains about your neck.

Prov. 4:1. Hear, my children, the instruction of a father, and give attention to know understanding.

Prov. 15:20. A wise son makes a father glad, but a foolish man despises his mother.

Prov. 20:20. Whoever curses his father or his mother, his lamp will be put out in deep darkness.

Ex. 21:17. And he who curses his father or his mother shall surely be put to death.

Gen. 9:24–25. So Noah awoke from his wine, and knew what his younger son had done to him. Then he said, "Cursed be Canaan; a servant of servants he shall be to his brethren."

[2] **Rom. 13:1.** Let every soul be subject to the governing authorities. For there is no authority except from God, and the authorities that exist are appointed by God.

1 Pet. 2:18. Servants, be submissive to your masters with all fear, not only to the good and gentle, but also to the harsh.

Rom. 13:2–7. Therefore whoever resists the authority resists the ordinance of God, and those who resist will bring judgment on themselves. For rulers are not a terror to good works, but to evil. Do you want to be unafraid of the authority? Do what is good, and you will have praise from the same. For he is God's minister to you for good. But if you do evil, be afraid; for he does not bear the sword in vain; for he is God's minister, an avenger to execute wrath on him who practices evil. Therefore you must be subject, not only because of wrath but also for conscience' sake. For because of this you also pay taxes, for they are God's ministers attending continually to this very thing. Render therefore to all their due: taxes to whom taxes are due, customs to whom customs, fear to whom fear, honor to whom honor.

Matt. 22:21. They said to Him, "Caesar's." And He said to them, "Render therefore to Caesar the things that are Caesar's, and to God the things that are God's."

[3] **Eph. 6:4, 9.** And you, fathers, do not provoke your children to wrath, but bring them up in the training and admonition of the Lord. ... And you, masters, do the same things to them, giving up threatening, knowing that your own Master also is in heaven, and there is no partiality with Him.

Col. 3:19, 21. Husbands, love your wives and do not be bitter toward them. ... Fathers, do not provoke your children, lest they become discouraged.

✠ **Prov. 30:17.** The eye that mocks his father, and scorns obedience to his mother, the ravens of the valley will pick it out, and the young eagles will eat it.

✠ **Deut. 27:16.** Cursed is the one who treats his father or his mother with contempt. And all the people shall say, "Amen!"

✠ **Deut. 32:46.** He said to them, "Take to your heart all the words with which I am warning you today, which you shall command your sons to observe carefully, even all the words of this law."

✠ **Prov. 13:24.** He who spares his rod hates his son, but he who loves him disciplines him promptly.

✠ **1 Tim. 2:1–2.** Therefore I exhort first of all that supplications, prayers, intercessions, and giving of thanks be made for all men, for kings and all who are in authority, that we may lead a quiet and peaceable life in all godliness and reverence.

✠ **1 Tim. 5:17.** Let the elders who rule well be counted worthy of double honor, especially those who labor in the word and doctrine.

✠ **Heb. 13:17–18.** Obey those who rule over you, and be submissive, for they watch out for your souls, as those who must give account. Let them do so with joy and not with grief, for that would be unprofitable for you. Pray for us; for we are confident that we have a good conscience, in all things desiring to live honorably.

LORD'S DAY 40

105. What does God require in the sixth commandment?

That I do not revile, hate, insult, or kill my neighbor either in thought, word, or gesture, much less in deed, whether by myself or by another,[1] but lay aside all desire of revenge;[2] moreover, that I do not harm myself, nor willfully run into any danger.[3] Wherefore also to restrain murder the magistrate is armed with the sword.[4]

[1] **Matt. 5:21–22.** You have heard that it was said to those of old, "You shall not murder, and whoever murders will be in danger of the judgment." But I say to you that whoever is angry with his brother without a cause shall be in danger of the judgment. And whoever says to his brother, "Raca!" shall be in danger of the council. But whoever says, "You fool!" shall be in danger of hell fire.

Matt. 26:52. But Jesus said to him, "Put your sword in its place, for all who take the sword will perish by the sword."

Gen. 9:6. Whoever sheds man's blood by man his blood shall be shed; for in the image of God He made man.

[2] **Eph. 4:26.** Be angry, and do not sin: do not let the sun go down on your wrath.

Rom. 12:19. Beloved, do not avenge yourselves, but rather give place to wrath; for it is written, "Vengeance is Mine, I will repay," says the Lord.

Matt. 5:25. Agree with your adversary quickly, while you are on the way with him, lest your adversary deliver you to the judge, the judge hand you over to the officer, and you be thrown into prison.

Matt. 18:35. So My heavenly Father also will do to you if each of you, from his heart, does not forgive his brother his trespasses.

[3] **Matt. 4:7.** Jesus said to him, "It is written again, 'You shall not tempt the Lᴏʀᴅ your God.'"

Rom. 13:14. But put on the Lord Jesus Christ, and make no provision for the flesh, to fulfill its lusts.

Col. 2:23. These things indeed have an appearance of wisdom in self-imposed religion, false humility, and neglect of the body, but are of no value against the indulgence of the flesh.

[4] **Ex. 21:14.** But if a man acts with premeditation against his neighbor, to kill him by treachery, you shall take him from My altar, that he may die.

✛ **Matt. 18:6–7.** Whoever causes one of these little ones who believe in Me to sin, it would be better for him if a millstone were hung around his neck, and he were drowned in the depth of the sea. Woe to the world because of offenses! For offenses must come, but woe to that man by whom the offense comes!

106. Does this commandment speak only of killing?

No, but in forbidding murder God teaches us that He abhors its very root, namely, envy,[1] hatred,[2] anger,[3] and desire of revenge; and that in His sight all these are hidden murder.[4]

[1] **Rom. 1:28–32.** And even as they did not like to retain God in their knowledge, God gave them over to a debased mind, to do those things which are not fitting; being filled with all unrighteousness, sexual immorality, wickedness, covetousness, maliciousness; full of envy, murder, strife, deceit, evilmindedness; they are whisperers, backbiters, haters of God, violent, proud, boasters, inventors of evil things, disobedient to parents, undiscerning,

untrustworthy, unloving, unforgiving, unmerciful; who, knowing the righteous judgment of God, that those who practice such things are deserving of death, not only do the same but also approve of those who practice them.

[2] **1 Jn. 2:9–11.** He who says he is in the light, and hates his brother, is in darkness until now. He who loves his brother abides in the light, and there is no cause for stumbling in him. But he who hates his brother is in darkness and walks in darkness, and does not know where he is going, because the darkness has blinded his eyes.

[3] **Jas. 2:13.** For judgment is without mercy to the one who has shown no mercy. Mercy triumphs over judgment.

Gal. 5:19–21. Now the works of the flesh are evident, which are: adultery, fornication, uncleanness, lewdness, idolatry, sorcery, hatred, contentions, jealousies, outbursts of wrath, selfish ambitions, dissensions, heresies, envy, murders, drunkenness, revelries, and the like; of which I tell you beforehand, just as I also told you in time past, that those who practice such things will not inherit the kingdom of God.

[4] **1 Jn. 3:15.** Whoever hates his brother is a murderer, and you know that no murderer has eternal life abiding in him.

✛ **Jas. 3:16.** For where envy and self-seeking exist, confusion and every evil thing are there.

✛ **Jas. 1:19.** So then, my beloved brethren, let every man be swift to hear, slow to speak, slow to wrath.

107. But is this all that is required: that we do not kill our neighbor?

No, for in condemning envy, hatred, and anger, God requires us to love our neighbor as ourselves,[1] to show patience, peace, meekness,[2] mercy,[3] and kindness[4] toward him, and to prevent his hurt as much as possible;[5] also, to do good even unto our enemies.[6]

[1] **Matt. 7:12.** Therefore, whatever you want men to do to you, do also to them, for this is the Law and the Prophets.

Matt. 22:39. And the second is like it: You shall love your neighbor as yourself.

[2] **Eph. 4:2.** With all lowliness and gentleness, with longsuffering, bearing with one another in love.

Gal. 6:1–2. Brethren, if a man is overtaken in any trespass, you who are spiritual restore such a one in a spirit of gentleness, considering yourself lest you also be tempted. Bear one another's burdens, and so fulfill the law of Christ.

Rom. 12:18. If it is possible, as much as depends on you, live peaceably with all men.

[3] **Matt. 5:7.** Blessed are the merciful, for they shall obtain mercy.

Lk. 6:36. Therefore be merciful, just as your Father also is merciful.

[4] **Rom. 12:10.** Be kindly affectionate to one another with brotherly love, in honor giving preference to one another.

[5] **Ex. 23:5.** If you see the donkey of one who hates you lying under its burden, and you would refrain from helping it, you shall surely help him with it.

[6] **Matt. 5:44–45.** But I say to you, love your enemies, bless those who curse you, do good to those who hate you, and pray for those who spitefully use you and persecute you, that you may be sons of your Father in heaven; for He makes His sun rise on the evil and on the good, and sends rain on the just and on the unjust.

Rom. 12:20–21. Therefore if your enemy is hungry, feed him; if he is thirsty, give him a drink; for in so doing you will heap coals of fire on his head. Do not be overcome by evil, but overcome evil with good.

✢ **Col. 3:12–14.** Therefore, as the elect of God, holy and beloved, put on tender mercies, kindness, humility, meekness, longsuffering; bearing with one another, and forgiving one another, if anyone has a complaint against another; even as Christ forgave you, so you also must do. But above all these things put on love, which is the bond of perfection.

✢ **Matt. 5:9.** Blessed are the peacemakers, for they shall be called sons of God.

Lord's Day 41

108. What does the seventh commandment teach us?

That all unchastity is accursed of God,[1] and that we should therefore loathe it with our whole heart,[2] and live chastely and modestly,[3] whether in holy wedlock or single life.[4]

[1] **Lev. 18:27–28.** For all these abominations the men of the land have done, who were before you, and thus the land is defiled, lest the land vomit you out also when you defile it, as it vomited out the nations that were before you.

[2] **Jude 22–23.** And on some have compassion, making a distinction; but others save with fear, pulling them out of the fire, hating even the garment defiled by the flesh.

[3] **1 Thess. 4:3–5.** For this is the will of God, your sanctification: that you should abstain from sexual immorality; that each of you should know how to possess his own vessel in sanctification and honor, not in passion of lust, like the Gentiles who do not know God.

[4] **Heb. 13:4.** Marriage is honorable among all, and the bed undefiled; but fornicators and adulterers God will judge.

1 Cor. 7:1–4. Now concerning the things of which you wrote to me: It is good for a man not to touch a woman. Nevertheless, because of sexual immorality, let each man have his own wife, and let each woman have her own husband. Let the husband render to his wife the affection due her, and likewise also the wife to her husband. The wife does not have authority over her own body, but the husband does. And likewise the husband does not have authority over his own body, but the wife does.

109. Does God forbid nothing more in this commandment than adultery and such gross sins?

Since both our body and soul are temples of the Holy Spirit, it is His will that we keep both pure and holy; therefore, He forbids all unchaste actions, gestures, words,[1] thoughts, desires,[2] and whatever may entice thereto.[3]

[1] **Eph. 5:3–4.** But fornication and all uncleanness or covetousness, let it not even be named among you, as is fitting for saints; neither filthiness, nor foolish talking, nor coarse jesting, which are not fitting, but rather giving of thanks.

1 Cor. 6:18–20. Flee sexual immorality. Every sin that a man does is outside the body, but he who commits sexual immorality sins against his own body. Or do you not know that your body is the temple of the Holy Spirit who is in you, whom you have from God, and you are not your own? For you were bought at a price; therefore glorify God in your body and in your spirit, which are God's.

[2] **Matt. 5:27–30.** You have heard that it was said to those of old, "You shall not commit adultery." But I say to you that whoever looks at a woman to lust for her has already committed adultery with her in his heart. If your right eye causes you to sin, pluck it out and cast it from you; for it is more profitable for you that one of your members perish, than for your whole body to be cast into hell. And if your right hand causes you to sin, cut it off

and cast it from you; for it is more profitable for you that one of your members perish, than for your whole body to be cast into hell.

[3] **Eph. 5:18–19.** And do not be drunk with wine, in which is dissipation; but be filled with the Spirit, speaking to one another in psalms and hymns and spiritual songs, singing and making melody in your heart to the Lord.

1 Cor. 15:33. Do not be deceived: "Evil company corrupts good habits."

LORD'S DAY 42

110. What does God forbid in the eighth commandment?

God forbids not only such theft[1] and robbery[2] as are punished by the government, but God views as theft also all wicked tricks and devices, whereby we seek to get our neighbor's goods, whether by force or by deceit,[3] such as unjust weights,[4] lengths, measures,[5] goods, coins, usury,[6] or by any means forbidden of God; also all covetousness[7] and the misuse and waste of His gifts.[8]

[1] **1 Cor. 6:10.** Nor thieves, nor covetous, nor drunkards, nor revilers, nor extortioners will inherit the kingdom of God.

[2] **1 Cor. 5:10.** Yet I certainly did not mean with the sexually immoral people of this world, or with the covetous, or extortioners, or idolaters, since then you would need to go out of the world.

[3] **Lk. 3:14.** Likewise the soldiers asked him, saying, "And what shall we do?" So he said to them, "Do not intimidate anyone or accuse falsely, and be content with your wages."

1 Thess. 4:6. That no one should take advantage of and defraud his brother in this matter, because the Lord is the avenger of all such, as we also forewarned you and testified.

[4] **Prov. 11:1.** Dishonest scales are an abomination to the LORD, but a just weight is His delight.

Prov. 16:11. Honest weights and scales are the LORD's; all the weights in the bag are His work.

[5] **Ezek. 45:9–10.** Thus says the Lord GOD: "Enough, O princes of Israel! Remove violence and plundering, execute justice and righteousness, and stop dispossessing My people," says the Lord GOD. "You shall have honest scales, an honest ephah, and an honest bath."

Deut. 25:13–15. You shall not have in your bag differing weights, a heavy and a light. You shall not have in your house differing measures, a large and a small. You shall have a perfect and just weight, a perfect and just measure, that your days may be lengthened in the land which the LORD your God is giving you.

[6] **Ps. 15:5.** He who does not put out his money at usury, nor does he take a bribe against the innocent. He who does these things shall never be moved.

Lk. 6:35. But love your enemies, do good, and lend, hoping for nothing in return; and your reward will be great, and you will be sons of the Most High. For He is kind to the unthankful and evil.

[7] **1 Cor. 6:10.** Nor thieves, nor covetous, nor drunkards, nor revilers, nor extortioners will inherit the kingdom of God.

[8] **Prov. 5:10.** Lest aliens be filled with your wealth, and your labors go to the house of a foreigner.

✢ **1 Tim. 6:10.** For the love of money is a root of all kinds of evil, for which some have strayed from the faith in their greediness, and pierced themselves through with many sorrows.

✢ **Jn. 6:12.** So when they were filled, He said to His disciples, "Gather up the fragments that remain, so that nothing is lost."

111. But what does God require of you in this commandment?

That I further my neighbor's good where I can and may, deal with him as I would have others deal with me,[1] and labor faithfully, so that I may be able to help the poor in their need.[2]

[1] **Matt. 7:12.** Therefore, whatever you want men to do to you, do also to them, for this is the Law and the Prophets.

[2] **Eph. 4:28.** Let him who stole steal no longer, but rather let him labor, working with his hands what is good, that he may have something to give him who has need.

✢ **Phil. 2:4.** Let each of you look out not only for his own interests, but also for the interests of others.

✢ **Gen. 3:19.** In the sweat of your face you shall eat bread till you return to the ground, for out of it you were taken; for dust you are, and to dust you shall return.

✢ **1 Tim. 6:6–7.** Now godliness with contentment is great gain. For we brought nothing into this world, and it is certain we can carry nothing out.

Lord's Day 43

112. What does the ninth commandment require?

That I bear false witness against no one,[1] twist no one's words,[2] be no backbiter or slanderer,[3] join in condemning no one unheard or rashly;[4] but that on pain of God's heavy wrath, I avoid all lying and deceit[5] as the very works of the devil;[6] and that in matters of judgment and justice and in all other affairs, I love, speak honestly, and confess the truth;[7] also, insofar as I can, defend and promote my neighbor's good name.[8]

[1] **Prov. 19:5, 9.** A false witness will not go unpunished, and he who speaks lies will not escape. ... A false witness will not go unpunished, and he who speaks lies shall perish.

[2] **Ps. 15:3.** He who does not backbite with his tongue, nor does evil to his neighbor, nor does he take up a reproach against his friend.

[3] **Rom. 1:28–30.** And even as they did not like to retain God in their knowledge, God gave them over to a debased mind, to do those things which are not fitting; being filled with all unrighteousness, sexual immorality, wickedness, covetousness, maliciousness; full of envy, murder, strife, deceit, evil-mindedness; they are whisperers, backbiters, haters of God, violent, proud, boasters, inventors of evil things, disobedient to parents.

[4] **Matt. 7:1–2.** Judge not, that you be not judged. For with what judgment you judge, you will be judged; and with the measure you use, it will be measured back to you.

Lk. 6:37. Judge not, and you shall not be judged. Condemn not, and you shall not be condemned. Forgive, and you will be forgiven.

[5] **Jn. 8:44.** You are of your father the devil, and the desires of your father you want to do. He was a murderer from the beginning, and does not stand in the truth, because there is no truth in him. When he speaks a lie, he speaks from his own resources, for he is a liar and the father of it.

[6] **Prov. 12:22.** Lying lips are an abomination to the LORD, but those who deal truthfully are His delight.

Prov. 13:5. A righteous man hates lying, but a wicked man is loathsome and comes to shame.

[7] **1 Cor. 13:6.** Does not rejoice in iniquity, but rejoices in the truth.

Eph. 4:25. Therefore, putting away lying, let each one of you speak truth with his neighbor, for we are members of one another.

[8] **1 Pet. 4:8.** And above all things have fervent love for one another, for love will cover a multitude of sins.

✣ **Jn. 7:24, 51.** Do not judge according to appearance, but judge with righteous judgment. ... Does our law judge a man before it hears him and knows what he is doing?

✣ **1 Pet. 2:21, 23.** For to this you were called, because Christ also suffered for us, leaving us an example, that you should follow His steps: ... who, when He was reviled, did not revile in return; when He suffered, He did not threaten, but committed Himself to Him who judges righteously.

✣ **Col. 4:6.** Let your speech always be with grace, seasoned with salt, that you may know how you ought to answer each one.

✣ **1 Pet 3:9.** Not returning evil for evil or reviling for reviling, but on the contrary blessing, knowing that you were called to this, that you may inherit a blessing.

Lord's Day 44

113. What does the tenth commandment require?

That not even the least inclination or thought against any commandment of God ever enter our heart, but that with our whole heart we continually hate all sin and take pleasure in all righteousness.[1]

[1] **Rom. 7:7–8.** What shall we say then? Is the law sin? Certainly not! On the contrary, I would not have known sin except through the law. For I would not have known covetousness unless the law had said, "You shall not covet." But sin, taking opportunity by the commandment, produced in me all manner of evil desire. For apart from the law sin was dead.

✣ **Prov. 4:23.** Keep your heart with all diligence, for out of it spring the issues of life.

✣ **Jas. 1:14–15.** But each one is tempted when he is drawn away by his own desires and enticed. Then, when desire has conceived, it gives birth to sin; and sin, when it is full-grown, brings forth death.

✣ **Matt. 15:11, 19–20.** Not what goes into the mouth defiles a man; but what comes out of the mouth, this defiles a man. ... For out of the heart proceed evil thoughts, murders, adulteries, fornications, thefts, false witness, blasphemies. These are the things which defile a man, but to eat with unwashed hands does not defile a man.

114. Can those who are converted to God keep these commandments perfectly?

No, but even the holiest men, while in this life, have only a small beginning of such obedience,[1] yet so that with earnest purpose they begin to live not only according to some, but according to all the commandments of God.[2]

[1] **1 Jn. 1:8–10.** If we say that we have no sin, we deceive ourselves, and the truth is not in us. If we confess our sins, He is faithful and just to forgive us our sins and to cleanse us from all unrighteousness. If we say that we have not sinned, we make Him a liar, and His word is not in us.

Rom. 7:14–15. For we know that the law is spiritual, but I am carnal, sold under sin. For what I am doing, I do not understand. For what I will to do, that I do not practice; but what I hate, that I do.

Eccl. 7:20. For there is not a just man on earth who does good and does not sin.

[2] **Rom. 7:22.** For I delight in the law of God according to the inward man.

Jas. 2:10–11. For whoever shall keep the whole law, and yet stumble in one point, he is guilty of all. For He who said, "Do not commit adultery," also said, "Do not murder." Now if you do not commit adultery, but you do murder, you have become a transgressor of the law.

✢ **Job 9:2–3.** Truly I know it is so, but how can a man be righteous before God? If one wished to contend with Him, he could not answer Him one time out of a thousand.

✢ **Ps. 19:13.** Keep back Your servant also from presumptuous sins; let them not have dominion over me. Then I shall be blameless, and I shall be innocent of great transgression.

115. Why then does God so strictly enjoin the Ten Commandments upon us, since in this life no one can keep them?

First, that as long as we live we may learn more and more to know our sinful nature,[1] and so the more earnestly seek forgiveness of sins and righteousness in Christ;[2] *second,* that without ceasing we diligently ask God for the grace of the Holy Spirit, that we be renewed more and more after the image of God, until we attain the goal of perfection after this life.[3]

[1] **1 Jn. 1:9.** If we confess our sins, He is faithful and just to forgive us our sins and to cleanse us from all unrighteousness.

Ps. 32:5. I acknowledged my sin to You, and my iniquity I have not hidden. I said, "I will confess my transgressions to the LORD," and You forgave the iniquity of my sin.

[2] **Rom. 7:24–25.** O wretched man that I am! Who will deliver me from this body of death? I thank God—through Jesus Christ our Lord! So then, with the mind I myself serve the law of God, but with the flesh the law of sin.

[3] **1 Cor. 9:24–25.** Do you not know that those who run in a race all run, but one receives the prize? Run in such a way that you may obtain it. And everyone who competes for the prize is temperate in all things. Now they do it to obtain a perishable crown, but we for an imperishable crown.

Phil. 3:12–14. Not that I have already attained, or am already perfected; but I press on, that I may lay hold of that for which Christ Jesus has also laid hold of me. Brethren, I do not count myself to have apprehended; but one thing I do, forgetting those things which are behind and reaching forward to those things which are ahead, I press toward the goal for the prize of the upward call of God in Christ Jesus.

✢ **Matt. 5:6.** Blessed are those who hunger and thirst for righteousness, for they shall be filled.

✢ **Ps. 51:12.** Restore to me the joy of Your salvation, and uphold me by Your generous Spirit.

The Lord's Prayer

LORD'S DAY 45

116. Why is prayer necessary for Christians?

Because it is the chief part of thankfulness which God requires of us,[1] and because God will give His grace and Holy Spirit only to those who earnestly and without ceasing ask them of Him, and render thanks unto Him for them.[2]

[1] **Ps. 50:14–15.** Offer to God thanksgiving, and pay your vows to the Most High. Call upon Me in the day of trouble; I will deliver you, and you shall glorify Me.

[2] **Matt. 7:7–8.** Ask, and it will be given to you; seek, and you will find; knock, and it will be opened to you. For everyone who asks receives, and he who seeks finds, and to him who knocks it will be opened.

Lk. 11:9–10, 13. So I say to you, ask, and it will be given to you; seek, and you will find; knock, and it will be opened to you. For everyone who asks receives, and he who seeks finds, and to him who knocks it will be opened. ... If you then, being evil, know how to give good gifts to your children, how much more will your heavenly Father give the Holy Spirit to those who ask Him!

Matt. 13:12. For whoever has, to him more will be given, and he will have abundance; but whoever does not have, even what he has will be taken away from him.

✢ **Eph. 6:18.** Praying always with all prayer and supplication in the Spirit, being watchful to this end with all perseverance and supplication for all the saints.

117. What belongs to such prayer which is acceptable to God and which He will hear?

First, that with our whole heart[1] we call only upon the one true God, who has revealed Himself to us in His Word,[2] for all that He has commanded us to ask of Him;[3] *second,* that we thoroughly know our need and misery,[4] so as to humble ourselves in the presence of His divine majesty;[5] *third,* that we be firmly assured[6] that notwithstanding our unworthiness, He will, for the sake of Christ our Lord, certainly hear our prayer,[7] as He has promised us in His Word.[8]

[1] **Jn. 4:22–24.** You worship what you do not know; we know what we worship, for salvation is of the Jews. But the hour is coming, and now is, when the true worshipers will worship the Father in spirit and truth; for the Father is seeking such to worship Him. God is Spirit, and those who worship Him must worship in spirit and truth.

[2] **Rom. 8:26.** Likewise the Spirit also helps in our weaknesses. For we do not know what we should pray for as we ought, but the Spirit Himself makes intercession for us with groanings which cannot be uttered.

1 Jn. 5:14. Now this is the confidence that we have in Him, that if we ask anything according to His will, He hears us.

[3] **Ps. 27:8.** When You said, "Seek My face," my heart said to You, "Your face, LORD, I will seek."

[4] **2 Chron. 20:12.** O our God, will You not judge them? For we have no power against this great multitude that is coming against us; nor do we know what to do, but our eyes are upon You.

[5] **Ps. 2:10.** Now therefore, be wise, O kings; be instructed, you judges of the earth.

Ps. 34:18. The LORD is near to those who have a broken heart, and saves such as have a contrite spirit.

Isa. 66:2. "For all those things My hand has made, and all those things exist," says the LORD. "But on this one will I look: on him who is poor and of a contrite spirit, and who trembles at My word."

[6] **Rom. 10:14.** How then shall they call on Him in whom they have not believed? And how shall they believe in Him of whom they have not heard? And how shall they hear without a preacher?

Jas. 1:6. But let him ask in faith, with no doubting, for he who doubts is like a wave of the sea driven and tossed by the wind.

[7] **Jn. 14:13–16.** And whatever you ask in My name, that I will do, that the Father may be glorified in the Son. If you ask anything in My name, I will do it. If you love Me, keep My commandments. And I will pray the Father, and He will give you another Helper, that He may abide with you forever.

Dan. 9:17–18. Now therefore, our God, hear the prayer of Your servant, and his supplications, and for the Lord's sake cause Your face to shine on Your sanctuary, which is desolate. O my God, incline Your ear and hear; open Your eyes and see our desolations, and the city which is called by Your name; for we do not present our supplications before You because of our righteous deeds, but because of Your great mercies.

[8] **Matt. 7:8.** For everyone who asks receives, and he who seeks finds, and to him who knocks it will be opened.

Ps. 143:1. Hear my prayer, O LORD, give ear to my supplications! In Your faithfulness answer me, and in Your righteousness.

✛ **Lk. 18:13.** And the tax collector, standing afar off, would not so much as raise his eyes to heaven, but beat his breast, saying, "God, be merciful to me a sinner!"

118. What has God commanded us to ask of Him?

All things necessary for soul and body,[1] which Christ our Lord comprised in the prayer which He Himself taught us.

[1] **Jas. 1:17.** Every good gift and every perfect gift is from above, and comes down from the Father of lights, with whom there is no variation or shadow of turning.

Matt. 6:33. But seek first the kingdom of God and His righteousness, and all these things shall be added to you.

✢ **1 Pet. 5:7.** Casting all your care upon Him, for He cares for you.

✢ **Phil. 4:6.** Be anxious for nothing, but in everything by prayer and supplication, with thanksgiving, let your requests be made known to God.

119. What is the Lord's Prayer?

"Our Father in heaven, hallowed be Your name. Your kingdom come. Your will be done on earth as it is in heaven. Give us this day our daily bread. And forgive us our debts, as we forgive our debtors. And do not lead us into temptation, but deliver us from the evil one. For Yours is the kingdom and the power and the glory forever. Amen."[1]

[1] **Matt. 6:9–13.** In this manner, therefore, pray: Our Father in heaven, Hallowed be Your name. Your kingdom come. Your will be done On earth as it is in heaven. Give us this day our daily bread. And forgive us our debts, As we forgive our debtors. And do not lead us into temptation, but deliver us from the evil one. For Yours is the kingdom and the power and the glory forever. Amen.

Lk. 11:2–4. So He said to them, "When you pray, say: Our Father in heaven, hallowed be Your name. Your kingdom come. Your will be done on earth as it is in heaven. Give us day by day our daily bread. And forgive us our sins, for we also forgive everyone who is indebted to us. And do not lead us into temptation, but deliver us from the evil one."

LORD'S DAY 46

120. Why did Christ command us to address God thus: "Our Father"?

To awaken in us at the very beginning of our prayer that childlike reverence for and trust in God, which are to be the ground of our prayer, namely, that God has become our Father through Christ, and will much less deny us what we ask of Him in faith than our parents refuse us earthly things.[1]

[1] **Matt. 7:9–11.** Or what man is there among you who, if his son asks for bread, will give him a stone? Or if he asks for a fish, will he give him a serpent? If you then, being evil, know how to give good gifts to your children, how much more will your Father who is in heaven give good things to those who ask Him!

Lk. 11:11–13. If a son asks for bread from any father among you, will he give him a stone? Or if he asks for a fish, will he give him a serpent instead of a fish? Or if he asks for an egg, will he offer him a scorpion? If you then, being evil, know how to give good gifts to your children, how much more will your heavenly Father give the Holy Spirit to those who ask Him!

✢ **1 Pet. 1:17.** And if you call on the Father, who without partiality judges according to each one's work, conduct yourselves throughout the time of your stay here in fear.

✢ **Isa. 63:16.** Doubtless You are our Father, though Abraham was ignorant of us, and Israel does not acknowledge us. You, O LORD, are our Father; our Redeemer from Everlasting is Your name.

121. Why is it added, "in heaven"?

That we might have no earthly thought of the heavenly majesty of God,[1] and from His almighty power expect all things necessary for body and soul.[2]

[1] **Jer. 23:23–24.** "Am I a God near at hand," says the LORD, "and not a God afar off? Can anyone hide himself in secret places, so I shall not see him?" says the LORD; "Do I not fill heaven and earth?" says the LORD.

Acts 17:24–25, 27. God, who made the world and everything in it, since He is Lord of heaven and earth, does not dwell in temples made with hands. Nor is He worshiped with men's hands, as though He needed anything, since He gives to all life, breath, and all things. ... so that they should seek the Lord, in the hope that they might grope for Him and find Him, though He is not far from each one of us.

[2] **Rom. 10:12.** For there is no distinction between Jew and Greek, for the same Lord over all is rich to all who call upon Him.

✢ **1 Kgs. 8:28.** Yet regard the prayer of Your servant and his supplication, O LORD my God, and listen to the cry and the prayer which Your servant is praying before You today.

✢ **Ps. 115:3.** But our God is in heaven; He does whatever He pleases.

LORD'S DAY 47

122. What is the first petition?

"Hallowed be Your name"; that is, grant us, first, rightly to know You,[1] and to sanctify, magnify, and praise You in all Your works, in which Your power, goodness, justice, mercy, and truth shine forth;[2] and further, that we so order our whole life, our thoughts, words, and deeds, that Your Name may not be blasphemed, but honored and praised on our account.[3]

[1] **Jn. 17:3.** And this is eternal life, that they may know You, the only true God, and Jesus Christ whom You have sent.

Matt. 16:17. Jesus answered and said to him, "Blessed are you, Simon Bar-Jonah, for flesh and blood has not revealed this to you, but My Father who is in heaven."

Jas. 1:5. If any of you lacks wisdom, let him ask of God, who gives to all liberally and without reproach, and it will be given to him.

Ps. 119:105. Your word is a lamp to my feet and a light to my path.

[2] **Ps. 119:137.** Righteous are You, O LORD, and upright are Your judgments.

Rom. 11:33–36. Oh, the depth of the riches both of the wisdom and knowledge of God! How unsearchable are His judgments and His ways past finding out! For who has known the mind of the Lord? Or who has become His counselor? Or who has first given to Him and it shall be repaid to him? For of Him and through Him and to Him are all things, to whom be glory forever. Amen.

[3] **Ps. 71:8.** Let my mouth be filled with Your praise and with Your glory all the day.

✠ **Ps. 100:3–4.** Know that the LORD, He is God; it is He who has made us, and not we ourselves; we are His people and the sheep of His pasture. Enter into His gates with thanksgiving, and into His courts with praise. Be thankful to Him, and bless His name.

✠ **Ps. 92:1–2.** It is good to give thanks to the LORD, and to sing praises to Your name, O Most High; to declare Your lovingkindness in the morning, and Your faithfulness every night.

✠ **Eph. 1:16–17.** [I] do not cease to give thanks for you, making mention of you in my prayers: that the God of our Lord Jesus Christ, the Father of glory, may give to you the spirit of wisdom and revelation in the knowledge of Him.

✤ **Ps. 71:16.** I will go in the strength of the Lord GOD; I will make mention of Your righteousness, of Yours only.

LORD'S DAY 48

123. What is the second petition?

"Your kingdom come"; that is, so govern us by Your Word and Spirit, that we submit ourselves to You always more and more;[1] preserve and increase Your Church;[2] destroy the works of the devil, every power that exalts itself against You, and all wicked devices formed against Your Holy Word,[3] until the fullness of Your kingdom come,[4] wherein You shall be all in all.[5]

[1] **Ps. 119:5.** Oh, that my ways were directed to keep Your statutes!

Ps. 143:10. Teach me to do Your will, for You are my God; Your Spirit is good. Lead me in the land of uprightness.

[2] **Ps. 51:18.** Do good in Your good pleasure to Zion; build the walls of Jerusalem.

Ps. 122:6–7. Pray for the peace of Jerusalem: May they prosper who love you. Peace be within your walls, prosperity within your palaces.

[3] **1 Jn. 3:8.** He who sins is of the devil, for the devil has sinned from the beginning. For this purpose the Son of God was manifested, that He might destroy the works of the devil.

Rom. 16:20. And the God of peace will crush Satan under your feet shortly. The grace of our Lord Jesus Christ be with you. Amen.

[4] **Rev. 22:17, 20.** And the Spirit and the bride say, "Come!" And let him who hears say, "Come!" And let him who thirsts come. Whoever desires, let him take the water of life freely. ... He who testifies to these things says, "Surely I am coming quickly." Amen. Even so, come, Lord Jesus!

Rom. 8:22–23. For we know that the whole creation groans and labors with birth pangs together until now. Not only that, but we also who have the firstfruits of the Spirit, even we ourselves groan within ourselves, eagerly waiting for the adoption, the redemption of our body.

[5] **1 Cor. 15:28.** Now when all things are made subject to Him, then the Son Himself will also be subject to Him who put all things under Him, that God may be all in all.

✣ **Ps. 102:12–13.** But You, O LORD, shall endure forever, and the remembrance of Your name to all generations. You will arise and have mercy on Zion; for the time to favor her, yes, the set time, has come.

✣ **Heb. 12:28.** Therefore, since we are receiving a kingdom which cannot be shaken, let us have grace, by which we may serve God acceptably with reverence and godly fear.

✣ **Rev. 11:15.** Then the seventh angel sounded: And there were loud voices in heaven, saying, "The kingdoms of this world have become the kingdoms of our Lord and of His Christ, and He shall reign forever and ever!"

✣ **1 Cor. 15:24.** Then comes the end, when He delivers the kingdom to God the Father, when He puts an end to all rule and all authority and power.

LORD'S DAY 49

124. What is the third petition?

"Your will be done on earth, as it is in heaven"; that is, grant that we and all men renounce our own will,[1] and without disputing obey Your will, which alone is good;[2] so that every one may fulfill his office and calling as willingly and faithfully[3] as the angels do in heaven.[4]

[1] **Matt. 16:24.** Then Jesus said to His disciples, "If anyone desires to come after Me, let him deny himself, and take up his cross, and follow Me."

[2] **Lk. 22:42.** ... "Father, if it is Your will, take this cup away from Me; nevertheless not My will, but Yours, be done."

Tit. 2:12. Teaching us that, denying ungodliness and worldly lusts, we should live soberly, righteously, and godly in the present age.

[3] **1 Cor. 7:24.** Brethren, let each one remain with God in that state in which he was called.

[4] **Ps. 103:20–21.** Bless the LORD, you His angels, who excel in strength, who do His word, heeding the voice of His word. Bless the LORD, all you His hosts, you ministers of His, who do His pleasure.

✣ **Rom. 12:2.** And do not be conformed to this world, but be transformed by the renewing of your mind, that you may prove what is that good and acceptable and perfect will of God.

✣ **Heb. 13:21.** Make you complete in every good work to do His will, working in you what is well pleasing in His sight, through Jesus Christ, to whom be glory forever and ever. Amen.

Lord's Day 50

125. What is the fourth petition?

"Give us this day our daily bread"; that is, be pleased to provide for all our bodily need,[1] so that we may thereby acknowledge that You are the only fountain of all good,[2] and that without Your blessing neither our care and labor, nor Your gifts, can profit us;[3] that we may therefore withdraw our trust from all creatures and place it in You alone.[4]

[1] **Ps. 104:27–28.** These all wait for You, that You may give them their food in due season. What You give them they gather in; You open Your hand, they are filled with good.

Ps. 145:15–16. The eyes of all look expectantly to You, and You give them their food in due season. You open Your hand and satisfy the desire of every living thing.

Matt. 6:25–26. Therefore I say to you, do not worry about your life, what you will eat or what you will drink; nor about your body, what you will put on. Is not life more than food and the body more than clothing? Look at the birds of the air, for they neither sow nor reap nor gather into barns; yet your heavenly Father feeds them. Are you not of more value than they?

[2] **Acts 14:17.** Nevertheless He did not leave Himself without witness, in that He did good, gave us rain from heaven and fruitful seasons, filling our hearts with food and gladness.

Acts 17:27–28. So that they should seek the Lord, in the hope that they might grope for Him and find Him, though He is not far from each one of us; for in Him we live and move and have our being, as also some of your own poets have said, "For we are also His offspring."

[3] **1 Cor. 15:58.** Therefore, my beloved brethren, be steadfast, immovable, always abounding in the work of the Lord, knowing that your labor is not in vain in the Lord.

Deut. 8:3. So He humbled you, allowed you to hunger, and fed you with manna which you did not know nor did your fathers know, that He might make you know that man shall not live by bread alone; but man lives by every word that proceeds from the mouth of the LORD.

Ps. 37:3–7, 16–17. Trust in the LORD, and do good; dwell in the land, and feed on His faithfulness. Delight yourself also in the LORD, and He shall give you the desires of your heart. Commit your way to the LORD, trust also in Him, and He shall bring it to pass. He shall bring forth your righteousness as the light, and your justice as the noonday. Rest in the LORD, and wait patiently for Him; do not fret because of him who prospers in his way, because of the man who brings wicked schemes to pass. ... A little that a righteous man has is better than the riches of many wicked. For the arms of the wicked shall be broken, but the LORD upholds the righteous.

[4] **Ps. 55:22.** Cast your burden on the LORD, and He shall sustain you; He shall never permit the righteous to be moved.

Ps. 62:10. Do not trust in oppression, nor vainly hope in robbery; if riches increase, do not set your heart on them.

✛ **Ps. 127:1–2.** Unless the LORD builds the house, they labor in vain who build it; unless the LORD guards the city, the watchman stays awake in vain. It is vain for you to rise up early, to sit up late, to eat the bread of sorrows; for so He gives His beloved sleep.

✛ **Jer. 17:5, 7.** Thus says the LORD: "Cursed is the man who trusts in man and makes flesh his strength, whose heart departs from the LORD. ... Blessed is the man who trusts in the LORD, and whose hope is the LORD."

✛ **Ps. 146:2–3.** While I live I will praise the LORD; I will sing praises to my God while I have my being. Do not put your trust in princes, nor in a son of man, in whom there is no help.

LORD'S DAY 51

126. What is the fifth petition?

"And forgive us our debts, as we forgive our debtors"; that is, be pleased, for the sake of Christ's blood, not to impute to us miserable sinners our manifold transgressions, nor the evil which always clings to us;[1] as we also find this witness of Your grace in us, that it is our full purpose heartily to forgive our neighbor.[2]

[1] **Ps. 51:1–4.** Have mercy upon me, O God, according to Your lovingkindness; according to the multitude of Your tender mercies, blot out my transgressions. Wash me thoroughly from my iniquity, and cleanse me from my sin. For I acknowledge my transgressions, and my sin is always before me. Against You, You only, have I sinned, and done this evil in Your sight—that You may be found just when You speak, and blameless when You judge.

Ps. 143:2. Do not enter into judgment with Your servant, for in Your sight no one living is righteous.

1 Jn. 2:1–2. My little children, these things I write to you, so that you may not sin. And if anyone sins, we have an Advocate with the Father, Jesus

Christ the righteous. And He Himself is the propitiation for our sins, and not for ours only but also for the whole world.

[2] **Matt. 6:14–15.** For if you forgive men their trespasses, your heavenly Father will also forgive you. But if you do not forgive men their trespasses, neither will your Father forgive your trespasses.

✠ **Ps. 51:5–7.** Behold, I was brought forth in iniquity, and in sin my mother conceived me. Behold, You desire truth in the inward parts, and in the hidden part You will make me to know wisdom. Purge me with hyssop, and I shall be clean; wash me, and I shall be whiter than snow.

✠ **Eph. 1:7.** In Him we have redemption through His blood, the forgiveness of sins, according to the riches of His grace.

Lord's Day 52

127. What is the sixth petition?

"And do not lead us into temptation, but deliver us from the evil one"; that is, since we are so weak in ourselves that we cannot stand a moment,[1] and besides, our deadly enemies, the devil,[2] the world,[3] and our own flesh,[4] assail us without ceasing, be pleased to preserve and strengthen us by the power of Your Holy Spirit, that we may make firm stand against them and not be overcome in this spiritual warfare,[5] until finally complete victory is ours.[6]

[1] **Jn. 15:5.** I am the vine, you are the branches. He who abides in Me, and I in him, bears much fruit; for without Me you can do nothing.

Ps. 103:14–16. For He knows our frame; He remembers that we are dust. As for man, his days are like grass; as a flower of the field, so he flourishes. For the wind passes over it, and it is gone, and its place remembers it no more.

[2] **1 Pet. 5:8–9.** Be sober, be vigilant; because your adversary the devil walks about like a roaring lion, seeking whom he may devour. Resist him, steadfast in the faith, knowing that the same sufferings are experienced by your brotherhood in the world.

Eph. 6:12–13. For we do not wrestle against flesh and blood, but against principalities, against powers, against the rulers of the darkness of this age, against spiritual hosts of wickedness in the heavenly places. Therefore take up the whole armor of God, that you may be able to withstand in the evil day, and having done all, to stand.

[3] **Jn. 15:19.** If you were of the world, the world would love its own. Yet because you are not of the world, but I chose you out of the world, therefore the world hates you.

[4] **Rom. 7:23.** But I see another law in my members, warring against the law of my mind, and bringing me into captivity to the law of sin which is in my members.

Gal. 5:17. For the flesh lusts against the Spirit, and the Spirit against the flesh; and these are contrary to one another, so that you do not do the things that you wish.

[5] **Matt. 26:41.** Watch and pray, lest you enter into temptation. The spirit indeed is willing, but the flesh is weak.

Mk. 13:33. Take heed, watch and pray; for you do not know when the time is.

[6] **1 Thess. 3:13.** So that He may establish your hearts blameless in holiness before our God and Father at the coming of our Lord Jesus Christ with all His saints.

1 Thess. 5:23–24. Now may the God of peace Himself sanctify you completely; and may your whole spirit, soul, and body be preserved blameless at the coming of our Lord Jesus Christ. He who calls you is faithful, who also will do it.

✣ **2 Cor. 12:7.** And lest I should be exalted above measure by the abundance of the revelations, a thorn in the flesh was given to me, a messenger of Satan to buffet me, lest I be exalted above measure.

128. How do you close this prayer?

"For Yours is the kingdom, and the power, and the glory, for ever"; that is, all this we ask of You, because as our King, having power over all things, You are willing and able to give us all good;[1] and that thereby not we, but Your holy name may be glorified for ever.[2]

[1] **Rom. 10:11–12.** For the Scripture says, "Whoever believes on Him will not be put to shame." For there is no distinction between Jew and Greek, for the same Lord over all is rich to all who call upon Him.

2 Pet. 2:9. Then the Lord knows how to deliver the godly out of temptations and to reserve the unjust under punishment for the day of judgment.

[2] **Jn. 14:13.** And whatever you ask in My name, that I will do, that the Father may be glorified in the Son.

Ps. 115:1. Not unto us, O Lord, not unto us, but to Your name give glory, because of Your mercy, because of Your truth.

129. What is the meaning of the word "Amen"?

"Amen" means: so shall it truly and surely be. For my prayer is much more certainly heard of God than I feel in my heart that I desire these things of Him.[1]

[1] **2 Cor. 1:20.** For all the promises of God in Him are Yes, and in Him Amen, to the glory of God through us.

2 Tim. 2:13. If we are faithless, He remains faithful; He cannot deny Himself.

✢ **Ps. 145:18–19.** The Lord is near to all who call upon Him, to all who call upon Him in truth. He will fulfill the desire of those who fear Him; He also will hear their cry and save them.

Now to Him who is able to do exceedingly abundantly
above all that we ask or think, according to the power
that works in us, to Him be glory in the church
by Christ Jesus to all generations,
forever and ever. Amen.
—*Ephesians 3:20–21*

Appendices

ಬ

After Question 129 the original edition of the Heidelberg
Catechism (1563) contained a number Scripture passages along
with the Apostles' Creed entitled, "Directory of principle texts on
how to properly learn the preceding Catechism." These texts are
used in the body of the Catechism.

Summary of the Law of God

ಬ

"Whence we come to know our sin and misery."

"You shall love the LORD your God with all your heart,
with all your soul, and with all your mind. This is the
first and great commandment. And the second is like it:
You shall love your neighbor as yourself. On these two
commandments hang all the Law and the Prophets."
—Matthew 22:37–40 [Deut. 6:5, Lev. 19:18] (Q4)

The Apostles' Creed

ಬಿ

"The articles of our Christian faith, or summary of the Gospel
from which we learn our redemption." (Q23)

I believe in GOD THE FATHER Almighty,
Maker of heaven and earth.

And in JESUS CHRIST,
His only-begotten Son, our Lord:
who was conceived by the Holy Spirit,
born of the virgin Mary,
suffered under Pontius Pilate,
was crucified, dead, and buried;
He descended into hell;
the third day He rose from the dead;
He ascended into heaven,
and sits at the right hand of
God the Father Almighty;
From there He will come to judge
the living and the dead.

I believe in the HOLY SPIRIT,
the holy, catholic Church,
the communion of saints,
the forgiveness of sins,
the resurrection of the body,
and the life everlasting.
Amen.

Institution of
the Sacraments

ও

"Institution of the holy sacraments through which the Holy Spirit
seals and assures us of this redemption."

Institution of Holy Baptism

Go therefore and make disciples of all the nations, baptizing
them in the name of the Father and of the Son and of
the Holy Spirit. He who believes and is baptized will be
saved; but he who does not believe will be condemned.
—Matt. 28:19, Mark 16:16 (Q71)

Institution of the Holy Supper of Christ

For I received from the Lord that which I also delivered to you:
that the Lord Jesus on the *same* night in which He was betrayed
took bread; and when He had given thanks, He broke *it* and
said, "Take, eat; this is My body which is broken for you; do
this in remembrance of Me." In the same manner *He* also *took*
the cup after supper, saying, "This cup is the new covenant in
My blood. This do, as often as you drink *it*, in remembrance of
Me." For as often as you eat this bread and drink this cup, you
proclaim the Lord's death till He comes.—1 Cor. 11: 23–26

And Paul in First Corinthians chapter 10 also says,

The cup of blessing which we bless, is it not the communion
of the blood of Christ? The bread which we break, is it not the
communion of the body of Christ? For we, *though* many, are
one bread *and* one body; for we all partake of that one bread.
—1 Cor. 10:16 (Q77)

The Law of God

&

"From which we learn how we should be thankful to God in our
whole lives for such blessings." (Q92)

And God spoke all these words, saying:

1. I am the LORD your God, who brought you out of the land of Egypt,
    out of the house of bondage. You shall have no other gods before
    Me.

2. You shall not make for yourself a carved image, or any likeness of
    anything that is in heaven above, or that is in the earth beneath, or
    that is in the water under the earth; you shall not bow down to them
    nor serve them. For I, the LORD your God, am a jealous God, visiting
    the iniquity of the fathers upon the children to the third and fourth
    generations of those who hate Me, but showing mercy to thousands,
    to those who love Me and keep My commandments.

3. You shall not take the name of the LORD your God in vain, for the
    LORD will not hold him guiltless who takes His name in vain.

4. Remember the Sabbath day, to keep it holy. Six days you shall labor
    and do all your work, but the seventh day is the Sabbath of the
    LORD your God. In it you shall do no work: you, nor your son, nor
    your daughter, nor your male servant, nor your female servant, nor
    your cattle, nor your stranger who is within your gates. For in six
    days the LORD made the heavens and the earth, the sea, and all that
    is in them, and rested the seventh day. Therefore the LORD blessed
    the Sabbath day and hallowed it.

5. Honor your father and your mother, that your days may be long
    upon the land which the LORD your God is giving you.

6. You shall not murder.

7. You shall not commit adultery.

8. You shall not steal.

9. You shall not bear false witness against your neighbor.

10. You shall not covet your neighbor's house, you shall not covet your
    neighbor's wife, nor his male servant, nor his female servant, nor his
    ox, nor his donkey, nor anything that is your neighbor's.

The Lord's Prayer

ಬ

"In which Christ Himself teaches us to show our gratitude
especially towards God, and to obtain from Him all the needs
of our bodies and souls." (Q119)

Our Father in heaven,

Hallowed be Your name.

Your kingdom come.

Your will be done on earth

    as it is in heaven.

Give us this day our daily bread.

And forgive us our debts,

    as we forgive our debtors.

And do not lead us into temptation,

    but deliver us from the evil one.

For Yours is the kingdom

    and the power

    and the glory forever.

Amen.

The Books of the Bible

ဆာ

OLD TESTAMENT BOOKS (39)

Genesis	Job	Isaiah
Exodus	Psalms	Jeremiah
Leviticus	Proverbs	Lamentations
Numbers	Ecclesiastes	Ezekiel
Deuteronomy	The Song	Daniel
Joshua	of Solomon	Hosea
Judges		Joel
Ruth		Amos
1 Samuel		Obadiah
2 Samuel		Jonah
1 Kings		Micah
2 Kings		Nahum
1 Chronicles		Habakkuk
2 Chronicles		Zephaniah
Ezra		Haggai
Nehemiah		Zechariah
Esther		Malachi

NEW TESTAMENT BOOKS (27)

Matthew	1 Timothy
Mark	2 Timothy
Luke	Titus
John	Philemon
The Acts	Hebrews
Romans	James
1 Corinthians	1 Peter
2 Corinthians	2 Peter
Galatians	1 John
Ephesians	2 John
Philippians	3 John
Colossians	Jude
1 Thessalonians	Revelation
2 Thessalonians	

Harmony with the
Three Forms of Unity

ℰ

Based on the order of the Heidelberg Catechism, this
harmony will aid in locating related statements of doctrine
found in the other confessions.

HEIDELBERG CATECHISM		BELGIC CONFESSION	CANONS OF DORT (RE = Rejection of Errors)
LD	Question	Article	Head & Article
1	1	---	1.12–14 ◆ RE 1.6–7 3-4.11 ◆ 5.8–12 RE 5.5
	2	---	1.1–4
2	3	---	3-4.5–6
	4	---	---
	5	14–15	3-4.3–6 ◆ 5.2–3
3	6	14	3-4.1
	7	14–15	1.1 ◆ 3-4.1–4
	8	14–15, 24	3-4.3–4
4	9	14–16	1.1 ◆ 3-4.1
	10	15, 37	1.4 ◆ 2.1 ◆ 3-4.1
	11	16–17, 20	1.1–4 ◆ 2.1–2
5	12	20	2.1
	13	14	2.2 ◆ 3-4.1–4
	14	---	---
	15	19	2.1–4
6	16	18–21	2.1–4
	17	19	2.1–4
	18	10, 18–21	2.1–4
	19	2–7	1.3 ◆ 2.5 ◆ 3-4.6–8
7	20	22	1.1–5 ◆ 2.5–7 ◆ 3-4.6
	21	23–24	3-4.9–14 ◆ RE 3-4.6
	22	7	1.3 ◆ 2.5 ◆ 3-4.6–8
	23	9	---

8	24	8–9	---
8	25	8–9	---
9	26	12–13	---
10	27	13	---
	28	12–13	---
11	29	21–22	2.3
	30	21–22, 24	2.5 ∙ RE 2.3–6
12	31	21, 26	---
	32	---	5.1–2
13	33	10, 18–19	---
	34	---	---
14	35	18–19, 26	---
	36	18–19	---
15	37	20–21	2.2–4
	38	21	---
	39	20–21	2.2–4
16	40	20–21	2.3–4 ∙ RE 2.7
	41	---	---
	42	---	---
	43	---	2.8
	44	21	2.4
17	45	20	RE 5.1
18	46	26	---
	47	19, 26	---
	48	19, 26	---
18	49	26	---
19	50	26	---
	51	---	2.8 ∙ 5.1–15
	52	37	---
20	53	11, 24	3-4.11–12 ∙ RE 3-4.5–8 ∙ 5.6–7
21	54	16, 27–29	1.1–18 ∙ 2.1–9 ∙ 5.9
	55	28, 30–31	---
	56	22–23	2.7–8 ∙ 5.5
22	57	37	---
	58	37	---
23	59	21–23	2.7–8

	60	21–23	2.7–8
23	61	21–23	2.7–8 • RE 2.4
24	62	23–24	2.1 • 3-4.3–6 • RE 3-4.4–5
	63	24	---
	64	24	3-4.11 • 5.12–13 • RE 5.6
25	65	24, 33	3-4.17 • RE 3-4. 7–9 • 5.14
	66	33	---
	67	33	---
	68	33	---
26	69	15, 34	---
	70	15, 34	---
	71	15, 24, 34	---
27	72	34	---
	73	34	---
	74	15, 34	1.17
28	75	35	---
	76	35	---
	77	35	---
29	78	35	---
	79	35	---
30	80	35	---
	81	35	---
	82	35	---
31	83	29–30, 32	---
	84	29, 32	---
	85	29, 32	---
32	86	24	3-4.11–12 • 5.10, 12
	87	24	---
33	88	24	3-4.11–12 • 5. 5, 7
	89	24	3-4.11–12 • 5.5, 7
	90	24	3-4.11–12 • 5.5, 7
	91	24–25	---
34	92	---	---
	93	---	---
	94	1	---
	95	1	---

35	96	32	---
35	97	---	---
	98	7	3-4.17 ⋅ 5.14
36	99	---	---
	100	---	---
37	101	36	---
	102	---	---
38	103	---	5.14
39	104	36	---
40	105	36	---
	106	---	---
	107	---	---
41	108	---	---
	109	---	---
42	110	---	---
	111	---	---
43	112	---	---
44	113	---	---
	114	24, 29	5.4
	115	25	3-4.17
45	116	---	---
	117	---	---
	118	---	---
	119	26	---
46	120	12–13, 26	---
	121	13	---
47	122	2, 7	---
48	123	36–37	---
49	124	12, 24	3-4.11, 16
50	125	13	---
51	126	15, 21–23	2.7
52	127	26	5.6–8
	128	26	---
	129	---	---

Outline of the Catechism
℘

This outline will help the reader to see the structure and flow of
the Catechism according to Lord's Days and Questions.

Introduction and Theme, LD1
> Our only comfort in life and death, Q1
> Three things needed to enjoy this comfort, Q2

THE GOSPEL

PART ONE: OUR MISERY (SIN)

Source of the Knowledge of our Misery, LD2
> Pedagogical work of the law, Q3
> Requirements of the law, Q4
> Our moral inability to keep the law, Q5

Man's Creation and the Fall, LD 3
> The creation of man, Q6
> Origin of human depravity, Q7
> Extent of human depravity, Q8

God's Justice and Mercy, LD 4
> Responsibility of man, Q9
> God's righteous judgment of sin, Q10
> The mercy and justice of God, Q11

PART TWO: OUR DELIVERANCE (SALVATION)

Need for Satisfaction, LD 5
> God's justice must be satisfied, Q12
> Human inability to make such satisfaction, Q13
> No creature whatever able to make satisfaction, Q14
> The sort of mediator required, Q15

The Only Mediator, Jesus Christ, LD 6
> Mediator needs a perfectly righteous human nature, Q16
> Mediator needs an omnipotent divine nature, Q17
> Identity of this mediator, Q18
> Source of knowing this: the Holy Gospel, Q19

THE APOSTLES' CREED

True Faith and Its Content, LD 7

Recipients of Christ's salvation, Q20

True faith defined, Q21

Essentials of faith, Q22

Twelve articles of the Creed, Q23

The Holy Trinity, LD 8

Three-fold division of the Creed, Q24

Revelation of the Trinity, Q25

GOD THE FATHER, *LD 9*

The Almighty Creator, Q26

Creation and Providence, LD 10

The providence of God, Q27

Benefits of divine providence, Q28

GOD THE SON, *LD 11*

The name Jesus, Q29

The only Savior, Q30

Three Offices of Christ, LD 12

His anointing as Christ: offices of Prophet, Priest, and King, Q31

The name "Christian," Q32

Deity and Lordship of Christ, LD 13

Jesus is the natural Son of God; Christians are adopted sons, Q33

His title Lord, Q34

Humanity of Christ, LD 14

Christ's incarnation: conception and virgin birth, Q35

How this profits us, Q36

Christ's Humiliation, LD 15

Christ's sufferings, Q37

Suffering judgment under Pontius Pilate, Q38

Significance of death by crucifixion, Q39

Christ's Death and Burial, LD 16

Necessity of suffering death, Q40

Christ's burial, Q41

Why Christians still suffer death, Q42

Practical benefits of the cross, Q43

Christ's descent into hell, Q44

Holy Baptism, LD 26
    How baptism assures us, Q69
    Meaning of baptism, Q70
    Institution of baptism, Q71

Value of Baptism, LD 27
    Outward washing is insufficient, Q72
    Biblical language for baptism, Q73
    Validity of infant baptism, Q74

The Lord's Supper, LD 28
    How the Lord's Supper assures us, Q75
    Meaning of the Supper, Q76
    Institution the Lord's Supper, Q77

Christ's Spiritual Presence at the Supper, LD 29
    Christ's presence by the Holy Spirit, Q78
    Biblical language for the Lord's Supper, Q79

Proper Participants at the Supper, LD 30
    Difference between the Lord's Supper and the Roman mass, Q80
    Who should come to the Lord's table, Q81
    Characteristics of unworthy partaking, Q82

Office of the Keys, LD 31
    Two keys of the kingdom, Q83
    The key of preaching, Q84
    The key of Christian discipline, Q85

PART THREE: OUR THANKFULNESS (SERVICE)

The New Life in Christ, LD 32
    Necessity of good works, Q86
    Impossibility of salvation without repentance, Q87

Two Parts of Sanctification, LD 33
    Two parts of true conversion, Q88
    Dying of the old man, Q89
    Making alive of the new man, Q90
    Good works defined, Q91
    The Law of God in the Ten Commandments, Q92

THE TEN COMMANDMENTS

First Commandment: Priority of God, LD 34
    Two tables of the Law, Q93
    Duties required, Q94
    Idolatry defined, Q95

Second Commandment: Spiritual Worship, LD 35
    Duties required: worship, Q96
    No images for worship, Q97
    No images in the church, Q98

Third Commandment: God's Name, LD36
    Duties required: oaths, Q99
    Misusing God's holy name, Q100

Oaths and Vows, LD 37
    Proper use of oaths, Q101
    No swearing by any creature, Q102

Fourth Commandment: Day of Rest, LD 38
    Duties required: the Lord's Day, Q103

Fifth Commandment: Authority, LD 39
    Duties required, Q104

Sixth Commandment: Life, LD 40
    Duties required, Q105
    Scope of the commandment, Q106
    Spiritual implications, Q107

Seventh Commandment: Purity, LD 41
    Duties required, Q108
    Spiritual implications, Q109

Eighth Commandment: Property, LD 42
    Sins forbidden: theft, Q110
    Duties required, Q111

Ninth Commandment: Truth, LD 43
    Duties required, Q112

Tenth Commandment: Contentment, LD 44
    Duties required, Q113
    Inability of Christians to keep the whole law perfectly, Q114
    Reasons God gave the commandments, Q115

THE LORD'S PRAYER

Prayer in the Christian Life, LD 45
Why prayer is necessary for Christians, Q116
Requisites for acceptable prayer before God, Q117
What God has commanded us to ask of Him in prayer, Q118
The Lord's Prayer, Q119

Preface to Prayer, LD 46
Addressing God as Father, Q120
Heavenly orientation, Q121

First Petition: God's Name, LD 47
Magnifying God's glory, Q122

Second Petition: God's Kingdom, LD 48
Promoting Christ's church, Q123

Third Petition: God's Will, LD 49
Seeking God's will, Q124

Fourth Petition: Daily Needs, LD 50
Provision for our needs, Q125

Fifth Petition: Forgiveness of Sins, LD 51
Confession of sin, Q126

Sixth Petition: Deliverance from Temptation, LD 52
Request for sustaining grace, Q127
Conclusion of prayer, Q128
Meaning of "Amen," Q129

65881271R00081

Made in the USA
Lexington, KY
27 July 2017